To Dr. Robert Smith, Jr.

Thank you for showing us the path of the wounded healer

Following God
for YOUTH
and young adults

BROKEN

When Life Falls Apart

A STUDENT BIBLE STUDY ideal for small groups
by David Rhodes & Chad Norris

🌸 **AMG** *Publishers*

Following God:
BROKEN Student Devotional Guide

Copyright © 2004 Wayfarer Ministries, Inc.

Published by AMG Publishers.

ISBN 0-89957-738-5

First printing: June 2004

Edited by: Robert Neely and Rick Steele

Interior Layout: Rick Steele

Cover design and interior design elements: Daryl Phillips and Jeff Belk at ImageWright Marketing and Design, Chattanooga, TN

Special thanks to: The Spencer and Hines families

Wayfarer Ministries
Box 201
1735 John B. White Sr. Boulevard
Suite 9
Spartanburg, SC 29301-5462
864-587-4985

Printed in the United States of America

08 07 06 05 04   –C– 6 5 4 3 2

web sites: www.wayfarerministries.org   www.amgpublishers.com

Table of Contents

BROKENNESS

Nobody wants it, yet most of us experience it. What are we supposed to do when life crashes down around us? Why does God allow his people to go through seasons of pain and misery? Could God have a purpose for these times of trial and confusion in our lives?

Job would answer "Yes" to these questions. Then he would go one step further and tell us to praise God through the pain. If there is any character in the Bible who knew brokenness, it was Job. But the greatest blessing in his life came in the midst of his suffering. His faith was stretched to limits many of us will probably never experience. But Job learned that in brokenness, we see God. In this book, we will learn the same.

Chad Norris and David Rhodes

...on using this Tips... devotional book

This student devotional book is intended to help you journey with Christ through the truth and impact of brokenness in your life.

Some of you are working through this study on your own, and some of you are going through this study in a group. Either way, this book is designed to take truths about brokenness and help you understand them, experience them and apply them to your daily life. Our hope is that, if you've gone through the devotions in the week leading up to your group time, you will be able to share your thoughts with the group and build on the things you learned during the week during that time. If you are going through this study on your own, we hope that you will take some time to enter into discussions with your friends, family and ministers about the things you are learning.

The book is divided into eight lessons with the purpose of allowing the reader to do one lesson per week for eight weeks. There are five devotional readings for each week's lesson. Although we have divided the devotions according to the five-day schedule, feel free to create your own schedule for completing your study.

Recognizing that there is no perfect structure for time alone with God, we have tried to produce devotions that are both varied and consistent. This book provides stories, questions, illustrations, background information, charts, and other tools to help illuminate the featured Scripture for each day and encourage and challenge your view of God.

Finally, at the end of each week, there is a notes page, which we hope you will use to take notes during your group session if you are going through Broken with others or to journal your own personal highlights from the week if you are going through the study on your own.

We believe this study will help you grow in your understanding of and trust in God, even in the midst of brokenness. Let the journey begin.

BROKEN

WEEK ONE

when life
falls apart

the reality
of brokenness

All of us go through hard times, times that make absolutely no sense. If you think about your past, you can certainly remember some painful and confusing times. Brokenness is no fun to talk about, but every one of us will experience it at some point in our lives. We will all be faced with the question of what to do when life falls apart.

■ **Describe a time of brokenness from your life.**

_____

_____

_____

_____

Read Job 1:1-19

The story of Job may seem a little extreme or distant to you. But people in our day experience brokenness that is just as life changing as Job's. A family in our community went through such a season of brokenness not that long ago. The mother agreed to share with us the story of how her family's life fell apart.

June 13, 2002, started out just like any other summer day in South Carolina, warm and beautiful. Clay, who had just turned twelve years old, was now officially part of the youth group at our church. He was supposed to be at [Boy] Scout camp, but after much debate he decided not to go. The group from church arrived for the first summer outing. Living on the lake is a true blessing, and entertaining was nothing new to Clay—he loved it. Everything was in order: the food was ready, the boats were clean, and the jet skis were gassed up. It was our first year to have the water trampoline, and we had even borrowed a banana boat from our neighbors to pull everyone around on.

As the first load took off on the banana boat, Clay was on the end. A group of us on the dock saw that someone had fallen off. It was Clay. We noticed a boat heading toward him, and then it appeared to hit him. I remember saying, "That boat just hit my child."

We just stood there frozen. As we started flagging down help I began to pray. For a second, thoughts of hospital-room breathing equipment ran through my mind, but then a feeling came over me and I knew it wouldn't be that way. I just prayed, "Lord, please be with Clay and don't let him suffer."

They yelled to call an ambulance, and we did. One of the adults in our group was a first responder and tried CPR. As the boat was pulling up to the dock with Clay, they told me to gather the kids and go inside. It was so quiet—no crying, no hysteria. We just went inside and sat in a circle on the floor, held hands and prayed.

When Clay's dad came inside, he looked at me and just shook his head. He had pulled Clay from the water, and it was his worst nightmare. The boat prop had struck and severed the main artery in Clay's neck, and he died instantly. We needed to be alone, and we wanted to run away. We couldn't let the kids see us lose it, so we went into another room and tried to piece together what had happened. The driver of the boat was a teenage girl, and although we had never met her, we would be forever connected. As we came out of the room, the kids sat there in their circle just looking at us. They didn't know. We had to tell them that their friend had died. We assured them that Clay was in good hands—he had given his heart to the Lord years earlier. We stressed that the person who needed our prayers now was the girl driving the boat.

Not long after that, they came and told us that she was downstairs and asked if we wanted to see her. We went and put our arms around her and cried together. After seeing her face, I remember saying, 'I forgive you.' A great girl from a good family, she like us was just out to have fun on the lake. The sun was in her eyes and she never saw Clay. Unlike the rest of us, her life had just changed forever over someone she had never even met.

We were all devastated—our family, our church, our community. Everything had changed. It seemed everyone was questioning God. I felt everyone questioning us and our reaction to our loss. How could a loving God have allowed this to happen? Why did these kids have to witness such a horrible scene? Why our church group? Why our family? We had worked so hard to make the perfect home with a stay-at-home mom and a successful, loving dad. Clay attended a Christian school.

The following morning, we were on the deck overlooking the lake. We wanted the world to stop. The squirrels, birds and traffic continued as if nothing had happened. It was at that point we realized it was just another day for everyone else.

- How do you feel after reading this story?

_____

_____

- What questions do you have for God after reading this family's experiences?

_____

_____

_____

In this book, we will ask some real and difficult questions about life and about God. Brokenness is real, and God's people should not shy away from this reality. God does not want us to hide our cares and concerns and act like things are always perfect. Instead, he wants us to come to him with everything in our lives, including times of brokenness.

We don't know whether you're in a season of brokenness now, have been through one in the past, or are thinking about how to deal with one whenever it comes. But whatever season you're in, this much is certain: God promises never to leave or forsake us. As the family in this story has learned, we are not promised an easy life or all the answers to life. But God is there in the midst of our brokenness. Over the next eight weeks, we'll see how that was true for Job and how it is true for us as well. Let's be honest as we begin a journey to find God in the midst of brokenness.

prayer exercise:

Open up to God today and be honest with him about the season you are in right now. Share from your heart about the brokenness you are in or have experienced. Know that God is there in the midst of your brokenness today.

reality
or religion

Last week I realized something pretty disturbing about myself. I hate to admit it, and to be honest I'm a little embarrassed about it, but I am addicted to reality TV shows. After staying up till midnight to watch the first episode of *Survivor All-Stars* and recording an episode of *The Apprentice* just so I could watch the Duke-North Carolina basketball game with a clean conscience, it struck me: reality TV has changed my viewing habits.

The funny thing is that I never thought I would be one of the people who hovered around the TV waiting to see what my favorite character would do next. Sure, I've had favorite TV shows. Back in the 80s, sitcoms like *The Cosby Show* and *Family Ties* were Thursday-night staples. In the 90s melodramas such as *Beverly Hills 90210*, *Felicity*, and *Dawson's Creek* caught my attention. I know some of these shows may sound like the Nick at Nite™ schedule to you, but it was my life. But now, it seems there is something interesting on TV every night. Shows like *Survivor*, *American Idol*, *The Apprentice* and even *My Big Fat Obnoxious Fiancé* have something about them that lures me in. I can't help wanting to see what happens next.

I'm not the only one caught up in this fad. Thirty-seven million viewers tuned in to watch *Survivor All-Stars* after the Super Bowl in February 2004, and the trend does not show any signs of stopping. Every network seems to be offering something in the way of reality TV. Television entertainment has dramatically transformed before our eyes. It's not as simple as saying sitcoms are out and reality shows are in. There will always be sitcoms, and there have always been reality shows—*Candid Camera* and *America's Funniest Home Videos* are two examples of unconventional programming that aired long before current-day reality shows hit the big time. But something in the psyche of people today longs to see unscripted TV. We want to see real people in real-life situations, and we don't want the tension to be resolved in thirty minutes. We want to see them respond in true-to-life ways, not just in moments of reality. We want to see how people react and think about what we would do in these real situations.

In 586 B.C. the city of Jerusalem fell to the Babylonian Empire. While many prophets had foretold this catastrophe years before, no one could have been prepared for how devastating this moment would be for the Israelites. Their temple was destroyed. The Holy of Holies was desecrated. Families were torn apart. Many died. Children were taken to foreign lands. Food was scarce. Every imaginable evil had become reality for God's people, and God was nowhere to be seen. The writer of Lamentations (most think it was Jeremiah) watched this horrifying event and called out to God in the midst of it. His honesty is striking. While he admitted that Israel's brokenness was largely a result of its own sin, he did not hide his true emotions from his God.

Read Lamentations

(We encourage you to read as much of the Book of Lamentations as God's Spirit directs you today. It could be a verse, a chapter, the entire book or anything in between. Whatever portion of the text you decide to read, ponder its words intently.)

■ What emotions did you see in the book of Lamentations? (Check all that apply.)

☐ anger   ☐ frustration   ☐ despair
☐ regret   ☐ sadness   ☐ depression
☐ love   ☐ compassion   ☐ resentment
☐ resentment   ☐ sorrow   ☐ repentance

■ Are you surprised to find these emotions in the writing of one of God's prophets?

☐ yes
☐ no

Explain your answer.

_____

_____

_____

_____

■ What emotions do you share with the writer of Lamentations at this time in your life?

_____

_____

Sometimes we think we need to come to God with a script. Somewhere along the way, we got the idea that Christians make their way through times of brokenness like a politician reading from a teleprompter. We're never supposed to be angry, sad, or depressed. All our statements are crafted with spiritual talk of faith and hope. But Jeremiah shows us that we can be deeply spiritual and authentically real at the same time. Religion says we have to put on "the Christian face," but the reality about God is that God can handle **all** our emotions, and he is not offended when we question him in the midst of our brokenness. Today, we want you to know that you do not need to be disingenuous to be right with God. You do not have to have everything together in your brokenness to meet God in the midst of it. Instead, God encourages us to come to him as we are, not as we think we should be.

prayer exercise:

Take some time today to pour out your heart to God using this journaling exercise.

God, I feel:

_____

God, I don't understand:

_____

God, how could you:

_____

the problem
of brokenness

On December 26, 2003, an earthquake measuring 6.3 on the Richter scale struck southern Iran. Experts estimated that more than forty thousand people were killed by this tragedy. Media outlets around the globe showed images of desperate people crying, weeping, mourning, and looking for explanations.

Ironically, just a few days before, an earthquake of similar magnitude hit California. But instead of more than forty thousand dying, only nine people were killed in California. No one looked for explanations there, and to be honest, compared to the crowds in Iran, very few Californians seemed all that upset about the earthquake. The Californians considered the earthquake part of the risk that comes with living on or near a fault line.

The differences in preparation for earthquakes in Iran and California are interesting because of how they affected the impact of those disasters. Buildings in California are built to withstand strong tremors, while in Iran most of the buildings are not. But to me, the most important contrast in these situations was in the way people responded to the earthquakes. The vastly different reactions in California and Iran reminded me of the diverse ways people interpret the brokenness around them. How can one person see something coming from the hand of God and someone else see a similar event as merely the result of poor construction or bad decision-making? Who is right? How do we know?

The Bible never pigeonholes brokenness as a simple cause-and-effect relationship. Sometimes we experience brokenness because Satan is attacking us. Sometimes brokenness comes because we live in a broken world where broken people have been given freedom to make decisions and choices, even ones that ultimately bring more brokenness to the world and to people around them. Sometimes we experience brokenness as tests from God. Other times God sends brokenness into our lives to mature us as his followers. And often, the reasons are combinations of one or more of these factors.

■ What caused Job's brokenness?

_____

_____

_____

■ Do these verses bother you?
   ☐ yes
   ☐ no

Why or why not?

_____

_____

_____

■ How do you normally interpret brokenness in your life?

_____

_____

_____

The story behind the scenes of the book of Job is disturbing. We see God and Satan in a heavenly wager of sorts. In fact, it even seems as if God is the one who called Satan's attention to one of his favorite followers. Satan was given permission to afflict Job's family and then Job himself. By the end of chapter 2, Job was one of the most pitiful specimens of human life imaginable. Even worse, Job never became aware of how his struggles and decisions have impacted a world for countless ages. He could only see the brokenness in front of him.

In a similar way, we too will struggle with the causes of evil and brokenness in our lives. Whether the untimely death of a loved one, an injury to ourselves, the divorce of our parents or one of a million other things leaves our lives totaled, we, too, will struggle with the question of "Why?" The truth is, we may never get the answer we are looking for. We may live our entire lives in the ambiguity of why bad things happen to good people. But though we may not be sure of many things in our seasons of pain, we can be sure of the truth shown throughout the Bible that there is never a situation beyond God's reach. We may never know the **why** of brokenness, but we can know the **who** of brokenness. We can trust God's hand whether he leads us to these times or simply leads us through them. Either way, when we leave our seasons of brokenness with our hands in his, we will know that he is good.

prayer exercise:

Take a moment to reflect on the brokenness you have experienced in your past. Have you been able to trace God's hand even in the worst of times? Reflect on these events and God's involvement in your life for a few minutes today as you again learn to trust him with the brokenness you are feeling right now.

Paul's
hardships

Many of us come into a relationship with Jesus with faulty expectations of a life of ease. We think that life with Jesus is free from hardships. But that's simply not true. Jesus promises never to leave us, but being a follower of Christ means that our life has more obstacles, not fewer. Our enemy Satan roars about seeking to devour God's people, and one of his biggest lies to us is that following Christ means never facing hardships.

Read Acts 16:6-24

The book of Acts is filled with stories of the apostle Paul's life and travels as he took the message of the gospel all over the world. But in this passage, we see something interesting happen. God led Paul to Philippi. However, when Paul got there, he found himself in a crisis.

- What happened to Paul in Philippi?
  - ☐ Everyone welcomed him.
  - ☐ The church grew without opposition.
  - ☑ He was beaten and thrown in jail.

- Are you surprised that Paul experienced a crisis when he went where God called him?
  - ☐ yes
  - ☐ no

- Are Christians exempt from struggles and pain in life?
  - ☐ yes
  - ☑ no

Why or why not?

_____

_____

_____

The prominent truth in this passage is that anyone who gives his life to Jesus will undoubtedly face opposition. We often hear that God's will is the safest place on earth, yet following God may lead us into brokenness. This brokenness is evident in Paul's life based on the events recorded in Acts 16. He did exactly what the Spirit of God led him to do, and he almost died as a result.

God never promised Paul that he would not endure hard times, but he did promise to be with Paul in the midst of those hard times. Paul's life was marked by beatings, imprisonment, shipwrecks and death threats, but he continued to follow God even when it led to pain and hurt.

Brokenness is a reality for everyone—even Christians. In fact, as we observe in Paul's example, following Christ can lead us into pain, suffering, and hard times. When hard times befall us, we need to take on the attitude of Paul and focus on God instead of on our brokenness. That doesn't mean we pretend we're not hurting. It simply means we look to God in the midst of our brokenness. In Day Five, we'll see how Job did this.

prayer exercise:

Tell the Lord that you don't expect an exemption from hard times. Ask him to remind you of his presence in the midst of whatever you're going through. Promise to follow him in spite of your feelings of brokenness. Spend some time focusing on the truth about who God is today.

Job

worshiped

This week, we've seen how life sometimes falls apart. As you read the story of Job, the story of Paul, the lamentations of Jeremiah and the story of the family mentioned in Day One, you had to confront some thorny issues that are not always easy to think about. We don't like to focus on our pain and brokenness, but all of us go through these times. In these times of brokenness, we are forced to ask some important questions.

■ What does a person's response to brokenness reveal about his/her relationship with God?

_____

_____

_____

■ Why does God give us a choice about how to respond to him during hard times?

_____

_____

_____

■ How do we make that choice?

_____

_____

_____

From a reading of Job 1, it appears likely that Job was confounded with many questions. As we saw at the beginning of the week, Job suffered the kind of brokenness most of us can only imagine. Today, we see his response.

Read Job 1:20-22

Fill in the blanks:
In Job 1:21, Job said, "The _Lord_ gave and the _Lord_ has taken away; may the name of the _Lord_ be _praised_."

■ How would you describe Job's response?

❑ normal   ❑ amazing
❑ surprising   ❑ foolish

This is one of the most remarkable passages in the entire Bible. Many people exist with the attitude of "What's in it for me?" But Job didn't operate this way. In the midst of devastating brokenness, Job didn't curse God; he chose to worship. He was undoubtedly confused, hurt, sad, and angry. But in the midst of all this, he chose to worship.

■ How would you have responded in Job's situation?

_____

_____

_____

Too often, Christians live by the question, "What can God do for me?" We love to follow God on our terms. As long as everything goes smoothly in our lives, we jump in and follow God without reservation. But when things don't go as we want them to go, we throw up our hands and get angry with God. Today, we see in Job's example a different way. Job lost everything, yet continued to worship the Lord. What a powerful testimony! Job's commitment to God in the midst of brokenness shows us how we can choose to respond to our brokenness.

Spend some time worshiping God. This may not be natural or easy for you; it certainly wasn't for Job. But today you can choose to follow God on his terms, not yours. Play a worship CD and honor God with heartfelt praise today.

This page is designed to give you space to take notes during your "Broken" group session or to journal your reflections on the highlights of this week's study.

WEEK TWO

the opportunity
of brokenness

1-2-07PP KP

from bad
to worse

Job 2:1-9

Being a Chicago Cubs fan is tough—at least, that's what they say. I'm not a Cubs fan, but I can sympathize with their struggles. Being a Cubs fan is a recipe for heartache and despair. The team hasn't won a World Series since 1908 and hasn't even been to the World Series since 1945, when according to legend, a restaurant owner put a curse on the team because it wouldn't let him bring a billy goat to a World Series game. While the Cubs have had a few glimpses of greatness, they are known much more for their seasons of despair and defeat.

But what makes the Cubs unique is that, despite all the heartbreaks and struggles over the years, they have some of the most loyal fans in all of sports. Wrigley Field continues to draw millions of fans each year, and the fan base always has a wait-till-next-year optimism about their team.

So you can imagine the euphoria Chicago has when the Cubs are successful. They got ever so close to the World Series in October 2003. The Cubs won their division in the final days of the season and then shocked the Atlanta Braves in the first round of the playoffs. The entire city of Chicago had come to a stand-still. It seemed like the billy goat curse might finally die, because all that stood between the Cubs and the World Series were the Florida Marlins, a low-budget cinderella story that had been playing so poorly early on that they fired their manager in mid-season. The Cubs took a three-games-to-two lead in the series and returned to Chicago needing to win just one more game to finally make it to the World Series. Even people who weren't baseball fans got excited about seeing history. It seemed like "next year" was finally here.

Tickets to Game Six were precious commodities that only the truest of Cub fans could afford. Steve Bartman was one of those die-hards. Like so many, he had cheered for the Cubs through thick and thin. But if Steve had known what would have happened in Game Six, he never would have gone. The bad parts of being a Cub fan suddenly got worse for Steve.

Steve had great seats right next to the field on the third-base line. He cheered with the rest of the Cubs fans as the home team took a 3-0 lead into the eighth inning. The Cubs were just six outs away from the World Series. But suddenly, the billy goat curse landed right on Steve Bartman. With one out and one man on base, Florida's Luis Castillo hit a foul ball down the line. Steve noticed that the ball was headed right toward him. Like any fan, Steve reached out to grab the souvenir. He was so focused on the ball that he failed to see Cubs leftfielder Moises Alou, who made his way toward the stands to try to catch the ball. In an instant, though, Steve reached for the ball, interfering with Alou's attempt to catch it, and the ball fell to the ground instead of being the second out of the inning. The second chance started a rally in which the Marlins scored eight runs and went on to win the game.

Steve entered Wrigley Field that night as a fan, but he left as a scapegoat. In a matter of minutes, Steve began to feel the wrath of fans who took out fifty years of frustration on him. He had to be escorted from the stadium by security, and after the Cubs lost Game Seven the next night, Steve had to go into seclusion usually reserved for someone in the witness protection program. Steve apologized, but Cubs fans would not forgive him. In one night, Steve went from Cubs fan to scapegoat. He never meant to cause trouble. He had acted like any excited fan would have. In fact, he really didn't do anything wrong. Major League Baseball rules prohibit fans from reaching out of the stands into the field of play to catch foul balls. But Steve didn't violate this rule because the ball had clearly entered the seating area. Nevertheless, Steve was in the wrong place at the most inopportune time. In one moment, his life bottomed out.

Read Job 2:1-9,10

■ How does Job's life go from bad to worse in this passage?

_____

_____

■ How would you have responded if this had happened to you?

_____

_____

_____

Just when you thought Job's life was bad enough, things went from bad to worse. Job had not sinned. In fact, his righteousness had brought him to this point. In chapter 2, Job's brokenness becomes even more personal as something far worse than the billy goat curse landed right on top of him. His body was covered with painful boils. All he could do was sit on a dung hill and scrape his boils with a sharpened piece of pottery. Even his wife turned against him. Job had worshiped God in his brokenness, but things kept getting worse.

It's hard to swallow this turn of events. You would think because Job worshiped in the midst of brokenness, God would have stepped in and changed his circumstances. But exactly the opposite happened, and this befuddles readers of Job to this very day. Job was seeking God, but his life still went from bad to worse. This is the hard truth of brokenness we come face-to-face with today. Worshiping in the midst of brokenness doesn't guarantee that things will change instantly. In fact, they may even get worse. This is life in the real world, a world with no easy answers and no quick deliverance.

prayer exercise:

Spend some time reflecting on what it means to follow God using the questions below.

- Have you ever followed God and tried to do the right things only to see your life disintegrate even further?

  ☐ yes *What's the most "unfair" thing that has*
  ☐ no   *ever happened to you?*

How did you handle that situation?

_____

_____

_____

How did it affect the way you thought about God?

■ What questions about God did you ask during this time?

_____

_____

_____

■ What encouragement did you find?

_____

_____

_____

Job 13:15 Though He slay me, yet will I hope in Him; I will surely defend my ways to His face.

Resolutions: with Gods empowering help of the Holy Spirit to

• do whatever is most to Gods Glory!
• do my duty, for the good of mankind in general.
• Never do anything, which I should be afraid to do, if it were the last hour of my life.
• To study the Scriptures steadily, constantly, and frequently.
• Ask myself at the end of every day, week, month, and year if I could possibly have done better.
• Until I die, not to act as if I were my own, but entirely and altogether Gods!

God can do what he wants

Matthew 20:1-16

Read Matthew 20:1-16

What's your reaction to this story?

☐ It's not fair. Those who worked all day got shafted.

☐ I guess it's fair, because everyone got what he was promised.

☐ God was really generous and gracious.

It's obvious from God's word that he truly loves his people. Love drove him to the cross, and his love is evident throughout our lives. The more we think about his love, the more our love for him grows. But even with this good news, it's easy for us to fall into a trap. We often forget that God is God, and we are not. God is sovereign, and he can do whatever he wants to do.

It's a problem when we try to follow God on our own terms. We come into our relationships with God with certain expectations. Our expectations are similar to the ones the all-day workers had in this parable in Matthew 20, and then we grumble when God doesn't act the way we want him to act. God never has to do anything we tell him to do. He is not our servant; he is our God who is supreme and stands above everyone and everything. He doesn't answer to us.

Many times, when we go through times of brokenness, we throw up our hands and start telling God how things are supposed to be. It's almost as if we want to give him orders. We may not come right out and say it like that, but we dwell on thoughts like, "That's not fair," or, "If I were God, I wouldn't do it that way." We must remember in our brokenness that our God has the authority and power to do whatever he wants to do and that his way is perfect.

Fill in the blanks:
In Matthew 20:14, the landowner says, "Take your pay and go. I _____ to _____ the man who was hired last the same as I _____ you."

Today, we focus on the words "want" and "give." It is God's prerogative to give whatever he wants to give. In times of frustration and brokenness, when we can't put the pieces of our lives together, we tend to tell God how displeased we are with him. As we saw last week, the **why** of brokenness can be a dead-end road. But as we wrestle with the **who** of brokenness, we must accept God's authority. God is God, and we are not. He can go about doing things however he wants to do them.

God will listen to our why questions. He hears our laments. But as believers in Christ, when we think about the **who** of brokenness, we need to come to an attitude of respect and submission. We can come before God and say, "This is your world. My life is yours. I'm going to follow you no matter what. You are God, and I am not." While all our questions may not be answered, we can trust that the God who is in control of our brokenness is a God who loves and cares for us.

■ How do you see this passage differently after going through this devotion?

_____

_____

_____

_____

prayer exercise:

Spend some time focusing and meditating on how big God is. Praise him for how awesome and huge he is. Confess that he is your God and you are his servant. Submit to his gracious hand today.

God never
changes

When I was a kid, my friends and I played a game where we would pretend to punch each other. It was a simple game: we'd stand about a foot apart, load up, and throw right hooks at each other's heads. The point of the game was to stand completely still as someone's fist came hurtling toward your face. More often than not, someone would flinch when the fist came toward him. That's when the fun began. When you made someone flinch, you got to slap him twice across the back. For ten-year-old boys, this was the greatest game ever.

■ **What drives your relationship with God?**
- ☐ my emotions
- ☐ what other people tell me about him
- ☐ what I read about him in his Word

Explain your answer.

_____

_____

_____

_____

The truth about us is that we often flinch in our relationships with God. Our emotions change and influence the way we act. We could wake up happy or bored or depressed or excited depending on the day. While some of us are more emotional than others, all of us can relate to this phenomenon. We all flinch.

Emotions are not bad. God created us to have emotions. But he never intended our emotions to drive our relationships with him. Jesus is our best picture of who God is. The more you read about Jesus in the Bible, the more you see that nothing catches him off guard. He never flinches at anything. No matter what Scripture records him doing or what is happening around him, people could always trust Jesus to act in line with his character. His steadiness and consistency shows us the unchanging nature of God. And because God's character never changes, he is an anchor for those who follow him.

Read Psalm 102

Fill in the blanks:
Psalm 102:27 says, "But you _____ the _____, and your _____ will never _____."

■ What suffering does the psalmist describe in these verses?

_____

_____

_____

■ What does the psalmist say about the character of God?

_____

_____

_____

■ How does this truth affect our everyday lives?

_____

_____

_____

_____

In times of pain and brokenness, we find ourselves experiencing emotions we could never have imagined. It's almost impossible to explain what brokenness feels like. The thing that sustains us as our emotions change constantly is the unchanging nature of God. No matter how we feel at any given moment, and no matter what our circumstances are, we can focus our attention on who God is and what he is like. As we'll see in the coming weeks, Job did this often throughout his journey of brokenness.

■ How does the truth that God never changes comfort you in your brokenness?

_____

_____

_____

_____

prayer exercise:

Take some time to thank God for his unchanging character. You may want to write him a letter that lists his unchanging attributes and praises him for them. Praise your solid rock. As you do, rest in the truth about him and find yourself being made whole by his stability.

BROKEN: THE OPPORTUNITY OF BROKENNESS

what time
is it?

Every year around Halloween, we Americans say goodbye to Daylight Saving Time and obediently set our clocks back one hour. This transition messes me up every year. Don't get me wrong—I love the night we "fall back." It's awesome to get an extra hour of sleep. But for the rest of the winter, that hour wreaks havoc with my sleep schedule. Something about getting home in the dark plays with my mind. I like summer days when it's sunny until 8:30 p.m., because it seems like so much more can happen in a day. But when it gets dark at 4:30 in the afternoon, I feel sluggish and even lazy or sad. Some nights, 7 p.m. feels like 2 a.m. I'm ready to go to bed, and I can't believe the day is gone, but then I realize it's 7 p.m., and the only people going to bed are two or eighty-two.

I don't know what people did before they had clocks. I'd be out of whack all the time without one. I'd go to bed at 6 p.m. in the winter and 1 a.m. in the summer. Some days, I'd wake up at 2:30 a.m. ready to start the day. But my clock keeps me from living that way. When I wake up at 2:30 a.m., the clock tells me I need to go back to sleep instead of starting my day. In the winter, when I want to go to bed at 7:30 p.m., my clock tells me I need to finish my day. Living by the clock keeps me from living by what I feel.

Read 1 Samuel 17

■ What situation did the army of Israel face in this story?
- ☐ an ambush
- ☐ a storm
- ☐ a giant

■ What was the difference between the way the army saw the situation and the way David saw the situation?

_____

_____

_____

_____

■ Why do you think David saw this situation differently?

❑ He had seen God work in the past.
❑ He had learned to trust God in every situation of his life.
❑ Walking with God in trust had changed the way David saw everything.
❑ All of the above

This story is really a story of time. From the outside, it looked like it was 11 p.m. The night was dark as Goliath made his stand, and no one wanted to challenge him. But where everyone else saw a threat, David saw an opportunity. He was telling time not by what he felt but by what he knew about God. In other words, he trusted his clock. In Day Five we will see how Job did much the same thing in his brokenness.

As Christians, we know that what we see and what we feel are not all there is to life. Walking with God means learning to tell time and trust his hand. Facing brokenness and threats and hardship is not easy, and if we are not careful, we will lose our sense of God entirely. It's so much easier to trust what we can see. But in the midst of our brokenness, God continually asks us to be like David and venture to places beyond our sight and our feelings. That means learning to see brokenness not as a threat but as an opportunity to demonstrate that God really is our God and to let our faith lead us down a road only the faithful dare to travel.

Meditate on the following questions.

■ How do you see brokenness in your life?

❑ as a threat

❑ as an opportunity

■ What would it look like for you to embrace your brokenness, venture out in faith and trust God's heart even when you can't see his hand?

_____

_____

_____

_____

As you think about these questions, ask God's Spirit to continue his transforming work inside you. Ask him to help you see the opportunities in the brokenness you are facing.

embracing
the opportunity

*Job
2: 1-10*

The karaoke machine has brought stardom to the common person. People of all ages and singing abilities can sing for an audience as if they were Garth Brooks, Tony Bennett, or Britney Spears. What once was confined to the shower is now on center stage in restaurants and bars, at parties and in living rooms across the country, and America loves it. Think about it: one of our most popular shows, *American Idol*, is really just the world's largest karaoke party.

American Idol gives ordinary people an extraordinary opportunity. People who had never had an audience to sing to now get to sing in front of millions on television. And even the worst singer can become famous from this opportunity. Just ask William Hung, who in 2004 slaughtered Ricky Martin's "She Bangs" in an *American Idol* audition classic that even *Saturday Night Live* noticed. Hung-mania spread across the nation on the Internet, as more than 7.5 million people visited a fan Web site in the first two weeks. Millions of people fell in love with this engineering student who danced poorly and couldn't carry a tune but who "gave his best" and had "no regrets at all."

Many people today are looking for an audience. I heard an *American Idol* contestant express this thought as she tearfully said that her life's dream was for America to hear her sing. For her, in one moment, that dream became a reality.

There is a reason we discuss our need for an audience as we continue to look at brokenness. While brokenness may never get us an audience like *American Idol* could, our reactions to brokenness catch the world's attention. The unbelieving world rarely looks at our faith when our lives are going great. After all, who couldn't talk about faith in those circumstances? But in the moments when life falls apart—those 9-1-1 (or 9/11) moments—the world looks at us as Christians to see if what we said during good times will match what we really hold to during seasons of calamity.

Read Job 2:1-10

Fill in the blanks:
Job 2:10 says, "(Job said) 'Shall we accept _____ from God, and not _____?' In _____ this, Job did not _____ in what he _____."

■ Contrast Job's response to his wife's response.

_____

_____

_____

We started the week by looking at Job 2:1–9. We saw that even though Job continued to follow God, his situation only got worse. Questions about God's control, goodness, and concern must have flooded Job's mind. But nothing could prepare us for the statement of verse 10. In the midst of incredible brokenness, Job demonstrates to us how real his faith was. When we read this passage, we sometimes look down on Job's wife, but she merely shows us the typical human reactions to brokenness: anger, rebellion, control, and internalization. Job's reaction is atypical. It is supernatural, something only God could display through a person. Job's statement in verse 10 may be one of the greatest statements of faith in the Old Testament. Essentially, Job says that if God is God, shouldn't he have the right to do whatever he wants? And if we are not God, isn't it our obligation to accept whatever God gives, good or bad, and honor him regardless? Job shows us the better way of faith. Most of the time we have trouble following God through brokenness, but Job shows us that it is not only possible to grow in brokenness but also possible to thrive.

The opportunity of brokenness is that, when we are broken, we have the chance to demonstrate that God is really God in our lives. When we live in plenty, we can easily say that God is God. But when things get tough, we have the opportunity to show a watching world that what we say we believe is what we really do believe. Job trusted the character of God even when the actions of God seemed different than what he knew about God's character. Such trust in the midst of brokenness speaks loudly to a world of skeptics.

■ How can you demonstrate faith to the world around you in your seasons of brokenness?

_____

_____

_____

_____

prayer exercise:

Ask God today to make your journey through brokenness a testimony to the world around you. This does not mean asking God to make you fake— false Christian smiles and avoiding reality are not what God wants from us. Rather, in the midst of being real, ask God to show you what it means to deal with brokenness as a Christian. Ask him to open your eyes to the audience peeking in at your life. Beg him to overwhelm you with his supernatural grace so that you too can speak loudly about your faith with your life.

_____

_____

_____

_____

_____

_____

_____

_____

_____

_____

_____

_____

_____

    This page is designed to give you space to take notes during your "Broken" group session or to journal your reflections on the highlights of this week's study.

BROKEN

WEEK THREE

the silence of God

the loud
silence

If you have been on a mission trip or traveled outside the country, you know the frustration of the language barrier. You realize your helplessness as soon as you get off the airplane in a foreign land. Everyone you encounter speaks in a language you cannot understand. You have no idea where you're going because all the signs are in a different language. The money looks different, and you have to do math to figure out how much something costs. As a foreigner, you stick out like a sore thumb. You're vulnerable, and you know it, because natives could take advantage of you whenever they wanted. Your only hope is that the few words you know will get you through or that you at least have a trusty guide to lead you along the way.

But what if the guide doesn't come? You'd be helpless, unable to speak the language and therefore unable to buy food, find a hotel, or do any of the things necessary to survive. Imagine one day without a guide becoming two days or even a week. While you might be able to stumble through enough conversations using hand motions to get some food and find the restroom, pretty quickly you'd run out of money because you were such easy prey for people around you. You could yell, but no one would listen or understand. You'd be helpless and alone, without any money or any hope things would get better anytime soon.

Read Job 3

Fill in the blanks:
Job 3:24-26 says, "For _____ comes to me instead of _____; my _____ pour out like _____. What I _____ has come _____ me; what I _____ has _____ to me. I have no _____, no _____; I have no _____, but only turmoil."

■ What emotions do you see Job experiencing in this passage? (Check all that apply.)

☐ frustration   ☐ intimacy   ☐ anger
☐ despair   ☐ peace   ☐ anxiety
☐ joy   ☐ comfort   ☐ confusion

■ Have you ever experienced a grueling time when it felt as if God were silent?

☐ yes
☐ no

If so, explain that situation.

_____

_____

_____

One of the worst tortures a human can go through is being in solitary confinement. Just the mere thought of it gives me a feeling of claustrophobia. But worse than the physical pain of being cooped up in one place is the emotional pain of having no one with whom you can talk. Communicating with others is part of what it means to be human. The story of Job from chapter 3 to chapter 37 is a story of solitary confinement. He had friends around him, but all they seemed to accomplish was to tear him down further than he already was. While he had some conversations with others, when all was said and done, Job stood all alone. Even God was silent in Job's pain. When we read these chapters, we wonder why God didn't say anything. Couldn't he have at least let Job know why this brokenness was necessary? God's silence is deafening throughout this portion of the book of Job.

This week we hit the pause button and take some time to talk about the silence of God in our lives. Sometimes, just like Job, we cry out to God for hours, days, months, and even years but hear nothing, and we're left feeling as though we're speaking a different language. Helplessness fills our hearts, eyes and mouths, and we even begin to question God. Why would God lead us into these moments? What is God doing in these seasons of our lives? These are the questions we will think about as we look at the silence of God.

Spend some time today being as silent as possible. Only talk when someone talks to you and even then use as few words as possible. As you take part in this exercise for an hour (or even longer if you choose) notice the reaction of the people around you. Do they notice? Do they get frustrated with you? As you watch the way people handle your silence, meditate on the way that you handle God's silence in your life. Do you notice? Do you get frustrated? Do you question whether he cares for you? Let these truths guide you in your time alone with God today.

finding
purpose in silence

It's human nature to always want the easy way out. And if it's not human nature, it's at least my nature. When someone tells me a riddle, I want him to give me the answer right away. When I see someone do a magic trick, I want him to show me how it was done so I don't have to wonder about it. When I start a workout program, I want to see results within twenty-four hours. When I change my diet for nutritional reasons, I want to feel better right away. As much as I hate to admit it, most of the time I want what I want how I want it when I want it. I don't want to work hard or scrape or claw or exhaust myself. I want to sit on my couch and be served.

Today's truth, though, pushes me in a different direction. Few of the things I value come easily. Most of the time hard work, suffering, and pain are part of the process of gaining things of real value. And though I don't like to admit it or talk about it, I grow the most as a person in these moments of great sacrifice.

This week we are talking about the silence of God. Yesterday we sat in the desperation of the silence. Today we want to ask whether God has a purpose in the silence. Most of the time, when someone talks about the purpose of silence, the message is what we've been talking about today. It's true that God uses silence to mature us as people, grow us in relationship with him, and purify our motives and desires. But today, I want us to consider these truths alongside another truth that is rarely talked about as a reason for God's silence: Sometimes God is silent in order to draw our faith to the surface.

Read Matthew 15:21-28

Fill in the blanks:
Matthew 15:23 says, "_____ did not _____ a _____."

■ Does this story bother you at all?
❑ yes
❑ no

Why or why not?

_____

_____

_____

_____

■ **How do you expect Jesus to respond to the woman?**

_____

_____

■ **How are your expectations shattered by the way Jesus responded to the woman?**

_____

_____

_____

This passage in Matthew 15 and its parallel passage in Mark 7 contain one of my favorite stories in the entire Bible. Mark 7:24–30 tells us that Jesus was trying to get away from the crowds, probably for a little rest and relaxation, when all of a sudden a woman who found out Jesus was in her town forced her way to the place he was staying and asked him to heal her daughter. Given the Jesus many of us learned about in Sunday School—the felt-board, candy-coated figure who was always sweet and standing with arms wide open—we expect that Jesus would welcome her with open arms. Instead, we're shocked and surprised to read that Jesus seemed a little grumpy. First, he didn't say a word to her. Then Jesus made a comparison where he called her a dog. As Christians, when we read this Scripture, we have to question what Jesus was doing here. He simply doesn't look like what we have come to expect.

This story has bothered me for quite a while. In fact, for several years I have kept coming back to it. I just can't seem to get away from the picture of Jesus in this story. (If you are doing this study with a group, you will likely discuss this story further in your group time.) But the one thing I have held onto more than anything else is that, in Jesus' silence and seeming harshness, he was drawing the woman's faith to the surface. The disciples were standing around showing frustration with the woman. They wanted her to go home. She didn't belong, and they did, and they didn't want her in the circle, at least not at the moment. But Jesus saw in this woman a seed of faith the disciples needed in their lives. So as Jesus championed the disciples' cause, the woman kept on coming. And in her persistence, she broke through. Jesus then turned and championed her great faith, and the disciples had to be scratching their heads in bewilderment. In his silence, Jesus was giving this Canaanite woman time to show her faith to his disciples in order to show them what faith and cleanliness really look like.

The hope for today is that when God is silent in our lives he may be maturing us, purifying us, or teaching us that we can't treat him like a cosmic Santa Claus. Even more, when he is silent he may also be drawing our faith to the surface so that the world around us can see what faith in God really looks like.

prayer exercise:

Spend some time today resting in God's silence. I know that seems weird, but spend some time talking with God and telling him that you will be here with him no matter what. Whether he speaks or not, tell him that you will keep persevering. Then look to see if he is giving your faith time to rise to the surface. Who could your faith impact if you persevere in silence and even in pain? How would this silent resolve show your faith as real and genuine?

dark nights
and deserts

Something I've noticed over the years is that the people that teach me the most are people who have endured a lot of pain in their own lives and have seen God step into the middle of that pain to show them who he is. These people have experienced what sixteenth-century Christian mystic St. John of the Cross called "the dark night of the soul." The dark night is a season so full of brokenness that it causes you to wonder if you'll ever make it through. God seems distant; the enemy seems close; and you wonder if Christianity is all it's cracked up to be.

Hear me very clearly on this: if you take Jesus very seriously and give your life to him in absolute surrender, you will go through seasons where you will be tested about what you truly believe. As we've seen throughout this study, Job went through the dark night of the soul in dramatic ways. While your season may not be as intense as Job's, it's normal for Christians to go through their own dark nights where they wonder if God is who he says he is. Instead of running from these times, we need to embrace them, as Jesus did when he was led to the desert to be tempted.

Read Matthew 4:1-11

■ What did Jesus do when Satan tempted him?

❑ He let his emotions control his response.

❑ He stayed quiet and tried to ignore the temptation.

❑ He gave in to temptation and admitted he was not strong enough to bear it.

❑ He answered the temptation with the Word of God.

■ What is the significance of the fact that Jesus responded to temptation with Scripture?

_____

_____

_____

I've read this story many times, but only recently have my eyes really been opened to the power of Jesus' response. This temptation was very real. He had gone forty days without eating. He must have been completely exhausted and drained. Then Satan shows up and offers him food. Satan targets Jesus' physical weakness and tries to get him to give in. But Jesus stands firm and keeps speaking the words of God back to Satan. Of course Jesus is hungry and thirsty. Of course he is exhausted beyond belief. But still he chooses to be guided and directed by what God's word says.

We must not miss this truth. Seasons will come and go, and sometimes we will be tempted to wonder if what we believe about God is true. The question is whether we will respond as Jesus did. Another way of thinking of the dark night of the soul is to picture it as a desert, a dry place in our lives. Jesus is our example in dark nights and deserts. He lived above what his emotions told him and clung to the Word of God. That is our challenge as well, because this is what helps us pull through these times. God's Word is true. He is who he says he is. If you are struggling right now, sink your teeth into what God's Word says and start speaking as Jesus did.

prayer exercise:

You may be in a dark night or desert time right now. If so, relax. You are not alone. Countless saints through the ages have gone through tough and difficult situations as well. Call on God's name right now and share your heart with him. Dig into God's Word and meditate on the truths about who he is. Ask Jesus to help you respond as he did in your dark nights and deserts.

when
silence is good

My son is ten months old, and he is at the stage where he explores everything. He finds his way into every cabinet, drawer, nook, and cranny in our house. My wife and I can't take our eyes off him for two seconds, because he will end up somewhere he is not supposed to be.

Our house has a gas fireplace behind glass. At the flip of a switch, a beautiful fire appears. I love this fireplace because it's no hassle. And Sam is absolutely infatuated with it. He loves to watch it glow. Sam always wants to touch the glass in front of the fire, but the problem is that it heats up to about, oh, two million degrees when the fire is on. It's blazing hot.

Sam and I developed a routine that normally went like this: he went up to the fire, and I said, "No!" very loudly. Sam looked at me and then turned to touch the glass. I said, "No," and pulled him away. He cried for three seconds, and then we started all over. We did this routine constantly—until something happened that changed everything.

One day, when I turned away for two seconds, Sam touched the glass. I don't think I'll ever have to tell him again not to touch it. It was so hot, and it hurt him. He finally realized why I said "No." Now, Sam enjoys looking at the fire, but he doesn't try to touch it. Nothing teaches us as quickly as pain.

Read 1 Samuel 16

Fill in the blanks:
First Samuel 16:19 says, "Then Saul sent messengers to Jesse and said, 'Send me your son _____, who is with the _____.'"

■ Whom did Samuel anoint to become king in this chapter?
- ☐ Saul
- ☐ Jesse
- ☐ David

- Where was David when Saul called for him?
  - ☐ home
  - ☐ the palace
  - ☐ in the field tending sheep

- What do you think was going through David's mind as he tended sheep after he had been anointed king?

_____

_____

- How would you have felt in David's situation?
  - ☐ confused   ☐ impatient
  - ☐ angry   ☐ content

Think about this story for a moment. God had decided to make David the next king of Israel, picking him over all his older brothers. David was not the biggest or smartest, but God chose him anyway. You would think that after being anointed king, David would have been rushed to the palace to start his new life. But that's not what happened. Instead, David found himself right back in the field tending sheep.

The text doesn't tell us, but I believe David must have been confused. He had to wonder why the next king of Israel had to tend some measly sheep. David must have been lonely, and he probably wondered what God was doing. But David was learning to trust God in the shepherd's field. The Bible shows us that some important things happened for David there. In the next chapter, David killed the giant Goliath, using skills he learned in the field when wild animals attacked the sheep. My son learned about fire by touching it, and David learned about battles from facing them in the field. Before he went out to fight Goliath, David said he knew God could lead him to victory because he had done so in the field.

What we perceive as great pain, loneliness or silence can actually be an atmosphere where we learn great things about God. The hardest and most painful times can turn out to be blessings because they help us learn. Even when God seems to be silent, he is leading us and making us into the kind of people he wants us to be.

■ What is your shepherd's field?

_____

_____

_____

■ How can you trust God from your shepherd's field?

_____

_____

_____

prayer exercise:

Ask God to show you how you can see the brokenness you're going through much like David saw his time in the shepherd's field. Ask the Father to teach you no matter what season you are in now. Embrace the learning God has for you in the shepherd's field.

not silent
forever

The blockbuster film *Bruce Almighty* deals with the ups and downs of life and offers some pretty profound thoughts about God in the middle of Jim Carrey's slapstick comedy. Although the movie took criticism from many different angles, the central truths the comedy addresses deeply impacted many viewers. It's natural for us to question God and God's silence in the middle of hardship as Bruce did. But no one could have anticipated the response to one scene in the middle of the movie. God is reaching out to Bruce, and God's telephone number shows up on Bruce's beeper. Within a week of the movie's release, thousands of people were calling God's phone number that they had seen in the movie. The phone number was not an active one in the Buffalo, New York, area (the setting of the movie), but it was an active number in many other area codes. In fact, in Sanford, North Carolina, the number was for Turner's Chapel Church, which just so happened to be led by a pastor named Bruce. There were so many calls that the producers changed the number to a non-existent one for the DVD and VHS releases.[1]

Most of the people who called God's phone number probably didn't really expect to get God on the phone. But the fact that there were so many calls points to a deep desire inside all of us. We really want to hear from God. We wish it could be as simple as calling God on the phone. When we pour our hearts out to God for hours, months, and years at a time and hear nothing, it's pretty hard.

Thankfully, though, the stories of Job and others in the Bible tell us we are not alone. And even when we go through moments and seasons of silence with God, the one thing we can be sure of from the stories in the Bible is that at just the right time, in just the right place and in just the right way, God will speak. The silence will never last one moment longer than necessary.

> Read Mark 4:35-41

- In what situation did the disciples find themselves here?
  - ☐ a famine ☐ a battle
  - ☐ a terrible storm ☐ a trap

- What was Jesus doing in this situation?
  - ☐ teaching
  - ☐ healing
  - ☐ sleeping

- How would you have reacted to this scenario if you were the disciples?

_____

_____

_____

One of my mentors asked this question about this Bible story: "What do you do with a sleeping Jesus?" His answer was simple yet profound: "You thank God that he is in the boat." The disciples were in a terrible situation as rain, wind, and waves threatened to capsize their boat and leave them struggling for their lives. The disciples frantically did everything they could think of to keep the boat afloat. But while all this was going on, Jesus was sleeping. Can you imagine the scene? The silence of Jesus must have been deafening. The disciples must have questioned whether Jesus was in touch with what was going on. They must have marveled at how someone could sleep in the middle of a storm like this. They may have even been mad that he wasn't helping out. Surely they questioned whether Jesus even cared for their welfare.

So the disciples acted just as any of us would have. They woke Jesus up and made him aware of their situation. Their situation seemed helpless. But at just the right moment, in just the right way, Jesus stood up and spoke in a way that none of them would ever forget. His words, "Peace, Be still!" calmed the waves, wind, and rain. It showed his authority over even the most menacing of foes. Most of all, it showed his concern for his frightened followers.

The truth with which we end this week is that many of us need to hold on in the middle of silence. God will not always be silent. He will not leave us in silence one moment longer than necessary. At just the right time and in just the right way, he will speak. I don't know how long it will take. But I do know that no storm you are in is greater than his words.

prayer exercise:

What wind, waves, and rain do you need God to calm in your life right now? How have you been struggling "to keep the boat afloat"? If you are a Christian, take peace today in knowing you are not in your "boat" alone. Although he may be silent, know that God is there. Rest in the knowledge that at just the right time, in just the right place and in just the right way, he will speak.

notes

1. Cliff Vaughn, *Bruce Almighty* Stirs Phone Calls to God," http://ethicsdaily.com, 5-30-03.

This page is designed to give you space to take notes during your "Broken" group session or to journal your reflections on the highlights of this week's study.

BROKEN

WEEK FOUR

though he slay me

no matter
what

In 1997, I married a young lady named Wendy Nalls. I remember my wedding day like it was yesterday. She walked down the aisle looking so beautiful, and we joined hands and faced the preacher. As he was talking to us, I was thinking, "I'm about to commit the rest of my life to someone—the rest of my life!" At that moment, I ran in terror out the door and down the street to escape from the eight hundred people in that church.

Of course, I'm kidding. But the truth is I was struck that day with the tremendous commitment I was making to Wendy. We have a covenant agreement that says we will never leave each other for any reason. For better or for worse, we're going to be together forever.

■ How would you describe your commitment for God?

_____

_____

_____

_____

Many times we come to God with the wrong attitude. We all have times when we're interested in God primarily for what he can do for us. If you watch preachers on television, you'll hear them focus on what God provides. And while it's true that God provides a lot, we must not forget that life isn't about what we want; it's about what God wants.

It's not unusual for someone in a time of brokenness to bail out on God. As soon as the water gets a little hot, we turn and run. But every once in a while we come across a person who stands in there and shows that he is committed to God no matter what. Job was that kind of person.

Fill in the blanks
Job 13:15 says, "Though he _____ me, _____ will I _____ in him."

This is one of the first high points in the entire book of Job. Job had been dealt a hand in life most of us couldn't handle, but he declared that he would trust even if he were slain (or killed). It's amazing to see Job respond to brokenness this way.

■ **What is your typical response to brokenness?**

_____

_____

_____

■ **Could you respond to brokenness as Job did?**
 ☐ yes
 ☐ no

Why or why not?

_____

_____

_____

The natural question we have after reading this passage is how we can become people who respond to brokenness as Job did. I think the answer lies in taking the focus off us and putting it on God. Job could not answer the questions he had about what was happening in his life. I'm sure he was scared and at times felt like he had lost his way. But he still declared that he was committed to God and that he wasn't moving no matter what. Job wasn't going to run out on God. He was committed to his Creator even in the midst of a tragic time.

God is raising up a kingdom of believers who will declare they are following God and will not be moved by anything. Too often, we concentrate not on our commitment to God but on what he can do for us. But this passage reminds us that we have a role to play. God will not make us commit to him. As with Job, the choice is ours.

prayer exercise:

Ask God to open your eyes so you can see him as he really is. Focus on how awesome he is. Ask yourself how committed you are to him. As you close, take some time to express to the Father that you are committed to him no matter what.

Daniel 3

even if
he does not

Job isn't the only biblical character to take a stand for his beliefs in the midst of a difficult situation. The Bible is full of stories like this. Another one is found in the book of Daniel, where three teenagers named Shadrach, Meshach, and Abednego found themselves in a situation that threatened their very lives.

Read Daniel 3

■ How would you have reacted in this situation?

☐ I would have bowed down to the statue.

☐ I would have done all I could to skip the ceremony.

☐ I would have stood up to the king.

■ How do you think Shadrach, Meshach, and Abednego found the courage to answer the king as they did?

_____

_____

_____

Many of us tend to run and hide when we are faced with danger. But heroes take another approach, defying the odds and standing their ground no matter what comes their way. This is why most movies feature someone saving the day. We love these stories of heroic acts. But the truth is, most of these Hollywood endings aren't life-or-death situations. Even if the character is in peril, the actor playing the role has the help of stuntmen, computer graphics, and editing to make the situation safe. They're not real heroes like firefighters who rush into a burning building to save people in danger.

When a situation is truly life or death, it changes everything. Shadrach, Meshach, and Abednego weren't facing suspended driver's licenses, probation, or community service for disobeying the king; they faced death in the furnace. Remarkably, they still chose to stand up for God. Even more amazingly, they committed to follow God even if he didn't step in to save them. Whether God rescued them or allowed them to die, these three teenagers were going to follow and worship him. When hard times surrounded them, they did not run **from** God; they ran **to** him. What an amazing picture of faith!

In our times of brokenness, we find ourselves faced with the same question that faced Shadrach, Meshach, and Abednego. Will we worship God? Will we follow him even if he does not step in to change our situation?

■ How does this story make you feel?

❑ inspired ❑ inferior
❑ scared ❑ determined

■ Can you imagine following God regardless of the consequences as Shadrach, Meshach, and Abednego did?

❑ yes
❑ no

Why or why not?

_____

_____

_____

■ What would it mean for you to follow God even if he does not change your situation?

_____

_____

_____

Take a few moments to meditate on the phrase, "Even if he does not." Think through these words on a very personal level. Be completely honest as you think about your walk with God. Are you walking with him as these three teenagers did? After a few minutes, talk to your heavenly Father about your life. Tell him what he means to you.

counting
the cost

Luke
14:28-33

Many of us are great at starting things, but few of us are great at finishing the things we start. In fact, commitment has almost become a curse word in today's society. Our houses are lined with pictures and products demonstrating this fact. Whether it's the flute or guitar we had to have that now sits in the corner of our room, the weights and bench that now rust and collect dust in our garage or our last Bible study book that has two chapters completed and six left unfinished, most of us have a hard time completing anything.

Read Luke 14:28-33

Fill in the blanks
In Luke 14:28, Jesus says, "Suppose one of you wants to _____ a _____.
Will he not _____ sit down and _____ the _____ to see if he has enough _____ to _____ it?"

■ Put this passage in your own words in ten words or less.

_____

Every week on my way to church I drive by a house that grabs my attention. It's in a great neighborhood. The houses surrounding it are home to families. The community is immaculately landscaped: yards mowed, bushes trimmed, and sidewalks edged. It looks like a storybook neighborhood, except for this one house, which sticks out like a sore thumb. This house has been empty ever since I started driving by it on the way to church two years ago. The yard is overgrown. There's never been a car in the driveway or a "for sale" sign in the yard. As best I can tell, the house is a project started with the best of intentions but left incomplete because the cost of finishing it was not calculated.

Jesus uses a similar picture to talk about the life of someone who seeks to follow him. He cautioned the people eager to sign on the dotted line and start the project by telling them they had better not start with him at all if they were not ready to invest everything. Jesus is not something you buy on clearance at The Gap. He cannot be followed half-heartedly. Lukewarm commitment will not do. He's not looking for overeager starters who have a hard time following through. It would be better not to start at all.

■ **How do the words of Jesus in this passage make you feel?**

☐ cautious   ☐ scared   ☐ desperate
☐ nervous   ☐ careless   ☐ shocked

The Jesus of the Bible is very different than the felt-board, candy-coated figure many of us learned about in Sunday School. For one thing, he is much more blunt. He asks a lot more from us than we remember. He takes discipleship a lot more seriously than we often do. How many half-finished but now abandoned projects started in Christ's name do we see today? Think about how this half-hearted following causes many of the problems our world has with Christians. Does the world drive by our lives and see nothing but good intentions laid aside in favor of the same things everyone else follows? Does it have to be this way?

The answer from the book of Job and many other places in the Bible is that it is possible to invest everything with God. Sure, there will be places in our lives where we will still be works in progress. The grass will always need mowing, and the landscaping will eventually need new plants. But like Job, it is possible for us to say through the power of God's Spirit living in us that we will follow no matter what, even if he slays us.

■ **What would it cost you today to journey toward becoming a whole-hearted follower of God?**

_____

_____

_____

■ What could it possibly cost you to finish this journey over the rest of your life?

_____

_____

_____

prayer exercise:

Today we have purposely avoided asking you to make any decisions. We want you to focus on counting the cost of walking with God. Many times we jump into decisions to relieve tension we feel in the moment, and we act as though simply making the decision completes things. But once the tension is relieved, we forget that making a commitment should lead us to follow that commitment with our lives. So instead of making any commitments to God in our prayer time today, maybe we would be better off just spending a few moments asking him to show us how much following him will cost us.

a leap
in the light

Some of the greatest moments of my life up to this point have come on a soccer field. From the time I was a little guy, I dreamed of playing soccer in college or even playing soccer for a living. So when I went to college on a soccer scholarship, I was living out my dream. But less than a year into this dream, I hit a major pothole. In a summer practice session, I tore my anterior cruciate ligament. Before I knew it, I had to spend six months of my life rehabilitating my knee. What started out like any other night of fun had left me scarred—literally.

The six months of rehab opened my eyes to just how dangerous the sport I loved was. Before my injury, I had never noticed how many players wore knee or ankle braces. I had been fortunate enough never to have a serious injury, so the thought never entered my mind. But after my injury, I saw braces everywhere. How could I have missed this reality? Needless to say, my first trips back on the field left me with some pretty difficult decisions. Constantly reminded of the potential costs of playing by the knee brace digging into my left leg, I knew playing wholeheartedly would be much more difficult. Sometimes naiveté can be a blessing. But now that I was fully aware of the cost and knew what six months of rehab were like, leaping toward passion and reckless abandon was much harder.

Read Luke 9:18-27

■ Use the space below to draw an image that illustrates what Jesus is saying in these verses.

■ **How is following Jesus a leap in the light rather than a leap in the dark?**

_____

_____

_____

_____

_____

Jesus did not leave us to leap into the dark when he called us to be his followers. He made us fully aware right from the start how costly leaping after him could be to us. For those of us who have fallen short in the past and understand our own potential for shortcoming, the decision to follow after Christ comes with baggage. It's so easy to let the scars of past failures, or better yet, the scars of past persecution, keep us from pressing forward. As with my decision after my knee injury, there seems to be a lot more at stake.

The good news is that, as we learned in Week 3, with every threat there also comes an opportunity. Nothing is more inspirational than watching someone return to full form after an injury. Nothing is more uplifting to a team than getting one of its own back. And no feeling is better than finishing a game where despite the risk you accomplished something you never could have done sitting on the sideline. Job is inspirational because, as he sat on the dung hill, his commitment never wavered. Like an injured person carried off the field with arm raised vowing to come back and finish what was started, Job demonstrated that he would not stop short of giving God everything.

We know that many who read this book have been wounded in the past. Some of these wounds came from things you have brought upon yourself. Others came from things someone else did to you. Still other wounds came simply because you followed Christ. Whatever the cause, we want you to know today that you too have an opportunity to be inspirational—not just by making a decision to commit everything to God today, but by living that commitment out with all your life. Yes, you may finish the game wearing a knee brace. The dangers of persecution, whether physical or social, are real. But Jesus is worth it.

Take your prayer time on the road today. Go for a walk or drive until you find a cross that catches your attention. You may have to go to your church or a nearby church, or you may want to get creative. When you find a cross, spend some meditating on it by re-reading today's passage and thinking about the truths we have talked about this week.

Philippians
1:12-26

to die
is gain

In some of the most difficult times of my life, I remember thinking, "What if this season lasts forever?" Have you ever felt that way? Those of us who have been through a season of brokenness certainly have. Life can be very hard, and when you are not thinking correctly, it is easy to fall prey to the thought that things will never change for the better. Some people fall into hopelessness because they can't get a proper perspective on their situation.

When I was a child, my grandfather died. It hurt me deeply because we were very close. I didn't know how to sort through my feelings of grief. Because of that experience, I came to associate death with great pain. As I got older, I did all I could to avoid cemeteries or anything else associated with death. This experience of losing someone close to me caused a great deal of emotional brokenness in my life. Throughout my teenage years and into my 20s, I never dealt with this loss and pain. If I heard someone preach on death, I would squirm in my seat and silently pray that I would not have to deal with this subject.

It would be easier if we could ignore our issues, but we can't. I was eventually forced to take this issue to God and let him step into the middle of my brokenness and speak healing over it. The way God healed me is found in today's passage.

Read Philippians 1:12-26

■ How did Paul react to his own hard season?
 ❏ He ran from his problems.
 ❏ He faced them head on.

■ Why do you think Paul reacted that way?

_____

_____

_____

In this passage, we get an honest picture of Paul. He was going through a difficult time and struggling to survive. But in the middle of his brokenness, he wrote a marvelous description of what true hope is.

```
Fill in the blanks:
Philippians 1:21 says, "For to me, to _____
is _____ and to _____ is _____."
```

Paul truly knew the Lord Jesus Christ. You don't make a statement like the one above without having a relationship with Jesus. Paul was not just interested in Jesus; he passionately followed him. From this relationship, Paul declared that he did not care if he lived or died, because his life wasn't about him. It was about Jesus. God used this declaration in my life to show me a true perspective on death and the loss of my grandfather. The more I studied and meditated on passages like this one, the more I realized that no matter what happens, I'm still OK. Even if my brokenness ends in death, I'm still OK. This is not an easy thing to say, and it's even harder to believe, but it's true. Paul said that dying would not just be OK; it would be gain because of Christ.

There is no season of brokenness too big for God to enter. That's what Job realizes in chapter 13, and it's what Paul affirms in Philippians 1. We can come to the same conclusion. We can be people like Job and like Paul who stand and say, "To live is Christ and to die is gain."

prayer exercise:

Take your biggest fears and concerns to God. Open your heart to him and allow him to step into the broken areas of your life and speak his truth into them. If your brokenness is pain from the past, take it to him. If it is a season you are going through now, take it to him. Ask him to show you the truth about your situation. It's possible for you to say as Job and Paul did that, "No matter what, even to death, I'll follow you, Father."

_____

_____

_____

_____

_____

_____

_____

_____

_____

_____

_____

_____

_____

    This page is designed to give you space to take notes during your
"Broken" group session or to journal your reflections on the highlights of
this week's study.

BROKEN

WEEK FIVE

my redeemer lives

dead or alive

Job
19: 1-24

I was hard at work a couple of weeks ago when the following story came across my e-mail.

Worker Dead at Desk for Five Days

Bosses of a publishing firm are trying to work out why no one noticed that one of their employees had been sitting dead at his desk for **five days** before anyone asked if he was feeling OK.

George Turklebaum, 51, who had been employed as a proofreader at a New York firm for thirty years, had a heart attack in the open-plan office he shared with twenty-three other workers. He quietly passed away on Monday, but nobody noticed until Saturday morning when an office cleaner asked why he was still working during the weekend.

His boss Elliot Wachiaski said: "George was always the first guy in each morning and the last to leave at night, so no one found it unusual that he was in the same position all that time and didn't say anything. He was always absorbed in his work and kept much to himself."

A postmortem examination revealed that he had been dead for five days after suffering a coronary. Ironically, George was proofreading manuscripts of medical textbooks when he died.

The story caught me off guard for a few minutes. It's hard to imagine a guy being dead five days before anyone noticed or to imagine that people assumed this guy who never moved was just really into his work. We have good reason to be skeptical of a sensational story like this because it never actually happened; the story is nothing more than an urban legend. But the picture of the mythical George Turklebaum is still disturbing. He was dead, but everyone around him thought he was alive.

Read Job 19:1-24

In chapter 19, Job was for all practical purposes the opposite of George Turklebaum. George was a dead man whom everyone thought was alive. Here, Job was a living man who for all practical purposes looked as if he were dead. In this chapter, Job used seven pictures to illustrate his plight. He described himself as:

- an animal caught in a net
- a falsely accused criminal on death row
- a traveler detained at customs
- a king who has been dethroned
- a building that has been destroyed
- a tree that has been uprooted
- an army that has been ambushed

Job summarized his predicament with the haunting words, "I am nothing but skin and bones; I have escaped with only the skin of my teeth" (19:20). In other words, Job said he was a dead man walking, someone who, in the lyrics of a Creed song, was six feet from the edge and thinking maybe six feet is not so far down. And all his pain came without a response from God.

■ **What would you describe as the lowest point in your life?**

_____

_____

_____

■ **Describe your walk with God during that time.**

_____

_____

_____

Just a few chapters earlier in the book of Job, Job states he would remain faithful to God "though he slay me." Last week, we focused on the faith of this courageous resolve. But as we move on in our study, it appears as if God will take

Job up on his offer. Job's faith really was costing him everything, and he knew it.

The truth for us today is that, in a similar way, our faith with God may cost us everything. Walking with God does not make us immune from trouble, hardship, or brokenness. To be honest, following God often increases our risk of these things. But just as dawn always comes after the darkest part of night, in our darkest moments we also find our most glorious hope. Hang on, because daylight is not far off.

prayer exercise:

Today we encourage you to practice "hanging on" even when everything inside tells you to give up and let go. To experience this truth in prayer, find a sturdy bar in your house or at the local playground where you can do a pull-up. Spend a few moments in prayer as you physically hang on to the bar without your feet touching the ground. As you try to hold on as long as you can, let the emotional and physical pain remind you of your times of brokenness, and lift your heart up to God in the middle of that pain. If you can't find a bar, do this prayer exercise by simply holding your arms over your head as long as you can while you pray. As you feel your arms tiring, let this physical weakness and your determination be a physical illustration of your spiritual weakness and determination to hang onto God no matter what.

my
redeemer lives

I hate to admit it, but I'm an underground professional wrestling fan. It's not that I believe this form of wrestling is real. (For those of you who think it is, I don't want to burst your bubble, but the Tooth Fairy isn't real either.) But I do love the storylines. Wrestling matches pretty much follow the same storyline, or at least they used to before the WWE turned everyone into a superstar. It used to be that the star wrestler always had a catchy name like Sting, Hulk Hogan, The Rock,™ or "Nature Boy" Ric Flair. The star wrestler's opponent usually had a name that was, well, his name. And if your wrestling name is your real name, you're about to take a beating.

Now we all know that when The Rock wrestles Brian Flora (or whatever the ham-and-egger's name is) that Brian is going to lose. But rarely do you see The Rock take it straight to the no-name character. Normally, Brian has a few moments at the beginning of the match where he actually has the upper hand. For a moment, it looks as though The Rock will be upset. But then, as in all great wrestling storylines, there is a moment where everything changes. This is never more evident than in tag-team battles. One of the tag-team champions is getting beaten to a pulp by the ham-and-eggers. It gets so bad that you begin to think the no-names will win. But then, in a moment that turns the tables, the wounded champion drags himself into the corner and makes a tag that brings his partner into the ring. The partner cleans house. winning the battle his partner had been losing. The man in the corner changes everything.

Read Job 19:25-27:

Fill in the blanks:
Job 19:25 says, "I know that my
_____ _____, and that in the
_____ he will _____ upon the
earth."

What changed in Job's situation from verse 20 to verse 25?

When we left Job yesterday, he was hanging on for dear life. Today we come to the rest of the story. In the midst of clinging to life, Job came to a startling reality about what he needed. He did not hang on thinking his life was about to magically change for the better. He did not hang on in hopes that he could manage his situation or leverage it to help himself. Job hung on and called out to the only one who had the power to help him—his **redeemer**.

This is a pretty big transition for Job. In chapter 13, Job calls for an umpire. At this point, he feels that if only someone could officiate his life, call fouls and make things fair, he could then deal with his brokenness. In chapter 17, Job calls for an advocate. He feels that if someone got in his corner and championed his cause, he could make it through. If only a lawyer were there to plead his case, he would be acquitted and freed. But in chapter 19, Job's situation has gotten so bad that he knows his only hope isn't in an umpire or an advocate. His situation is so desperate that only a full-fledged redeemer can help.

The Hebrew word Job uses in 19:25–27 that is translated "redeemer" is *goel*, which literally means **kinsman redeemer**. It is the kind of redeemer Boaz was for Ruth. The kinsman redeemer was a close relative who would willingly buy back, free, or fill in for a family member in a desperate situation. In the case of death, this redeemer would marry the wife of the deceased relative so he could father a son who would carry on the dead man's name and family line. In other words, the kinsman redeemer would live for the person who had died.

In verse 25, Job expresses his trust in the Redeemer who will live no matter what Job's situation looks like. He is saying, "I know my situation looks desperate, but as my end approaches, I am calling out for someone who is big enough to do what only God can do." Job is struggling to the corner of the ring. We have seen him get pummeled for the first nineteen chapters. It looks as though he is going to lose. But verse 25 is the tag that changes everything. Here Job tags out of his life, and God steps into the center of Job's brokenness. In this moment, everything begins to change. Job didn't know when it would happen, but he knew he could trust his partner to live and stand in the end no matter what happened to him. It wasn't an instant deliverance, but Job did not need to fight for himself any longer. God had stepped to the center of Job's ring.

■ What would it look like for you to tag out of your life and let God step to the center of your ring in your season of brokenness?

_____

_____

_____

prayer exercise:

Take time today to think about a wrestling match. Consider the storyline we have discussed today and try to remember a match that paints the picture we've talked about. You may even choose to watch a tag-team match on TV or go to the video store to find a classic match to better illustrate this truth, if you can find a prayerful way to do it. As you focus on this picture, imagine yourself tagging out of your life and allowing God to step into the middle of your brokenness. Once you have allowed this picture to remind you of the truth of your Redeemer, put on a Christian worship CD and meditate on what you have read and seen today.

magnetic
personality

So far this week, we've seen how in the midst of his desperation Job declared that his Redeemer lives. Over the next three days, we're going to think in more detail about what a redeemer is.

All my life, I've been captivated by Jesus. I can remember being a little boy, about three years old, and telling my dad that I could not wait to spend forever with Jesus. I look back now and wonder how I knew at such an early age how incredible Jesus is.

There are not enough words in any language to describe how wonderful Jesus is. I can tell you from my journey over the years that Jesus is more than I could ever imagine. Jesus came to this earth and brought great news of healing, help, and hope. It's easy to see why we are drawn to Jesus in seasons of brokenness. He knows just what to say and how to say it.

Read Isaiah 61:1-3

■ What does this passage say is the common thread of Jesus' mission?

_____

_____

_____

■ Why is Isaiah 61:1-3 good news for you?

_____

_____

_____

In this passage we see what Jesus came to earth to do. It is incredible news – especially to those in seasons of brokenness. After Jesus returns to set up his new kingdom, we will spend eternity celebrating how Jesus spoke healing into the lives of his followers. There is no healer like Jesus. He is the master of taking the broken and making it whole.

■ **Have you ever been in a situation where you saw Jesus heal you?**

❑ yes
❑ no

If so, explain that situation.

_____

_____

_____

_____

One of the great temptations in our culture is for us to try to solve our issues on our own. We definitely live in a society that believes only the strong survive. But is that really true? It seems as though Christianity's message is that only the weak survive. The reason is that in spite of our weakness, Jesus is strong. He steps into our brokenness and calls us toward the road to healing, like a magnet draws metal to itself. The magnet is a beautiful picture of Jesus. He attracts the broken and the downtrodden. No matter where in life you find yourself, Jesus is there with his arms open to welcome you into his healing embrace.

A trip through the gospels shows us how Jesus is the master healer. He shows compassion for those who are hurting physically, emotionally, and spiritually. And since Jesus is the revelation of the true nature of God, we know that God is a God of healing. It is even one of his covenant names, **Jehovah Rapha**—the God who heals. If you are broken and life has beaten you up, you can rest in the fact that God is your healer, no matter what your situation or your emotions might say. Come to him with reckless abandon and let him heal you as only he can.

Be open and honest with God about your life. If you are in need of healing, tell him about it today. Maybe there is pain in your life that you've been carrying for a long time. If so, ask him to bring healing to that area. No pain is too big for Jehovah Rapha, the God who heals.

out of
the ravine

Do you have that friend who is always there no matter what? There's nothing like having a buddy who sticks by you through thick and thin and who is there to help you whenever and however you need it. When you know someone "has your back," you live more confidently and more victoriously.

When I was younger, I went to camp every summer with my church. As soon as we arrived, each of us had to partner up with a buddy. The counselors called it "the buddy system." The rules of the buddy system are pretty simple—you stay with your buddy all week. You share bunk beds, go to meals together, go to activities together, and always know where your buddy is. Whenever the counselors check attendance, you are responsible for knowing where your buddy is. Having a buddy makes a kid feel safe and connected even in an unfamiliar place like camp.

Read Hebrews 13:5-6

So many aspects of God's character are revealed in the fact that he is our Redeemer. Yesterday, we saw how our Redeemer heals us. Today, we turn to look at how our Redeemer helps us. It's pretty awesome to think about God as our helper. When we go through the ups and downs of life, we trust that he is right there beside us. As verse 5 says, he will never leave us under any circumstance.

■ How does it help you to know that God is always with you?

_____

_____

_____

A few years after I got married, I talked my wife into letting me buy a truck. I was so pumped about getting a vehicle that made me feel like a real man. I'm not sure what I thought I would do with my truck, but I knew I'd think of something. We settled on a Ford Ranger. I couldn't wait to take this awesome piece of machinery on some back roads so I could see what it would do.

You've probably already figured out that I was headed for trouble. It's funny what you'll do when you're caught up in the moment. But I took my new truck on some property behind our house to try it out. I felt like a cowboy on his horse exploring the western frontier. Everything was great for about three minutes—until I drove into a ravine. I tried everything I could think of for two hours, but I couldn't get the truck out of that hole. It was stuck.

I finally realized there was nothing I could do. I was getting worked up until a light came on inside my head and I thought, "I need to call Lynn." Lynn was a good friend of mine who would drop anything anytime to help me. He came out to find me in his bigger, better, manlier truck and pulled my truck out of the ravine pretty quickly. That night, I told my wife, "I don't know what I would have done if Lynn hadn't been there."

```
Fill in the blanks:
Hebrews 13:6 says, "So we say with
_____, 'The _____ is my
_____; I will _____ be
_____. What can man do to me?'"
```

■ How does it make you feel to know that you can call on God anytime and any place?
  ☐ relieved   ☐ overprotected
  ☐ confident   ☐ safe

■ Have you had an experience in your life where you realized God was your helper?
  ☐ yes
  ☐ no

If so, describe that situation.

_____

_____

_____

_____

What an awesome promise it is to know that God will never leave us! Even more, he is our helper. I can't imagine a better helper. He reaches down into the broken areas of our lives and gently pulls us out of the ravines we so often find ourselves in. Call on him. He is your helper.

prayer exercise:

Take some time to think about some times in your life when you saw God as helper. As you remember these times, praise God for being your helper.

Habakkuk 3

the
surviver tree

The book of Habakkuk was written during a time in Israel's history known as the exile. Years earlier, the nation of Israel had been divided into two kingdoms—a northern kingdom known as Israel and a southern kingdom known as Judah. By the time Habakkuk came on the scene, the Assyrians had already conquered and destroyed the northern kingdom. Now, God revealed to Habakkuk that the Babylonians would defeat the southern kingdom of Judah and ransack the capital city of Jerusalem. In today's passage, Habakkuk anticipated the brokenness of exile while trusting and hoping in God in the middle of it.

Read Habakkuk 3

■ Put Habakkuk 3:17-19 in your own words.

_____

_____

_____

■ What would it look like for you to find hope in brokenness in your life?

_____

_____

_____

A few months ago I was in Oklahoma City. This is kind of odd, because Oklahoma City is not a place someone would normally go on vacation or visit for fun, especially someone from the east coast. It is not on the way to anywhere a South Carolinian like me would likely drive. People like me only end up in Oklahoma City if they need to be there. That was the case for me, as I went there to do a retreat, talking to some students about the love of God.

The drive from the airport to the retreat center was an endless expanse of farmland. The sameness of the scenery around me bugged me because it seemed like a scene from a movie repeating itself over and over. So when I found out on the return trip that I had a couple of hours to burn, I wasn't that excited. But then I remembered a few moments in time when Oklahoma City was at the center of our nation's attention.

It happened on what at first seemed to be a normal day. But April 19, 1995, turned out to be anything but normal. At 9:02 a.m. central time, U.S. history changed when a truck bomb exploded outside the Murrah Federal Building in downtown Oklahoma City. In a matter of moments, half the building was gone. People who had been in meetings a moment before now found themselves at best covered in rubble. Confusion filled the air as one of our country's worst tragedies unfolded. In all, 168 people died as a result of the attack.

When I saw signs advertising the memorial to this event, I knew how I would spend my extra time in Oklahoma City. My time at the memorial was overwhelming as I journeyed through the experiences of that horrendous day by reading the stories and hearing the testimonies of those who survived the tragedy.

The memorial is flanked by barriers reading 9:01 (the minute before the tragedy) and 9:03 (the minute after the bomb exploded). The memorial captures the brokenness of 9:02. Eight years after the tragedy, I stood at 9:02 and witnessed the incredible brokenness.

In the middle of this brokenness, there was an incredible hope that took me by surprise. Story after story told of the goodness ordinary people showed in the midst of this tragedy. People waited in line to donate blood, risked their lives to save others, opened their homes and churches and volunteered their resources to help in any way possible. Hope and goodness stifled the brokenness.

The entire tour moved me in ways that are still fresh in my mind. But probably the most memorable thing was a reflection point known as the Survivor Tree. This tree is an eighty-year-old American Elm that bears witness to the violence of 9:02. It stood in a parking lot across from the disaster, surrounded by cars that were flipped or totaled by the blast. But somehow, in the middle of the chaos, the tree stood almost untouched. Now, this tree is in a reflection area, and there is a plaque with this quote: "The spirit of this city and this nation will not be defeated; our deeply rooted faith sustains us." I sat there that day moved to the point of tears looking at this tree and thinking about all it meant to those who had journeyed through this incredible moment of brokenness.

As I gathered myself to walk from under the branches of this old elm tree, I noticed a nest with some young birds above me. And as if God was standing there with me, I sensed the Spirit embedding this image in my mind. Here were a few birds making their home in this incredible tree. New life was now housed in this symbol of hope. Now whenever I hear of Oklahoma City, I don't think of a city in the middle of nowhere. I think of a place where brokenness gave way to hope.

As Christians, we too have a survivor tree. On this tree, the Savior of the world gave his life for our sins. On a regular yet not-so-normal day two thousand years ago, brokenness and hope stood side by side. In Jesus' brokenness we find hope. Today, God invites us to nest in the branches of this tree, though there may not be any buds on our fig trees or grapes on our vines. Even if the olive crop fails, the fields produce no food, and there are no sheep in the pen, Jesus invites us to hope in him. We take hope because not even death itself could stop Jesus from accomplishing his work for our world and in our lives. We take hope though our world falls apart because we know that our Redeemer lives.

prayer exercise:

Go online or to a library to find some stories about the Oklahoma City bombing and its aftermath. As you read these stories of hope and goodness in the midst of brokenness, allow God to minister to you in the midst of your brokenness. Try to be open to the Holy Spirit as he leads you to hear from God. Who knows? Perhaps you, too, will walk away today with an image driven in your mind by God's Spirit.

_____

_____

_____

_____

_____

_____

_____

_____

_____

_____

_____

_____

_____

   This page is designed to give you space to take notes during your "Broken" group session or to journal your reflections on the highlights of this week's study.

WEEK SIX

God speaks

thunder
and lightning

When I was growing up, our family took vacations to the beach every summer. We usually went to Hilton Head Island, South Carolina. My siblings and I always looked forward to playing miniature golf and riding golf carts at the theme park there. We also loved to go to Harbor Town, look at the sights and listen to the famous guitar player. There were so many great things to do. But one of my favorite things was sitting on the balcony of our condominium when a storm rolled in off the ocean. I remember sitting there and seeing for miles as storms came in over the water. The sky turned black, and lightning flashed all over the horizon. For a nine-year-old, this was an awesome sight.

It was one thing to see the storm miles away, but it was even more exciting to see the storm up close and personal. Sitting there as the thunder boomed and lightning flashed all around was like being in the tornado-chasing movie *Twister*. It's impossible to sit in that situation and pretend to be in control of it. I didn't know where the lightning would flash next or how long it would take the storm to get to us. I'd try to guess what was coming next, but I could never tell. All I knew for sure was that the storm was awesome, and it was headed my way.

■ **Have you ever waited on God to speak when it seemed like he never would?**

❑ yes
❑ no

If so, explain that situation. What did you do?

_____

_____

_____

■ Do we have any control over God?
 ❑ yes
 ❑ no

What is the significance of this truth for our lives?

_____

_____

_____

_____

Read Job 38—41

Job had been playing a waiting game. He had been sitting and waiting on God to speak. He had expressed everything he could to God through lament, questions, and even frustration. He had said all he could say. He had even tagged out of his life. So we can only imagine how miserable Job was.

But then suddenly, as if out of nowhere, God spoke into the middle of Job's misery. It may not have been the message Job was expecting or hoping for, but God was in control, not Job. And when God spoke, it was an awesome and powerful sight.

Fill in the blanks:
Job 38:1 says, "Then the _____ answered _____ out of the _____."

prayer exercise:

Spend some time meditating on this passage today. As you read how God spoke to Job, let God's words seep into your heart as well. Be open with God about whatever season you are in, and ask him to speak to you. Then wait. If God doesn't speak immediately, continue to be patient and wait for him. God spoke to Job in his time, and he'll speak to you in his time too.

the

whisperer

The movie *The Horse Whisperer* tells the story of Tom Booker and his fascinating gift for gentling horses. In the movie, Tom uses his calm, steady, gentle approach to heal scars that both a horse and a young girl got in a riding accident. In one scene, the skittish horse gets startled when a cell phone goes off. The horse runs off to the far end of a large pasture. Instead of chasing the horse, Tom walks into the pasture and sits down. For what seems like hours, he waits there, until the horse becomes curious and gradually comes to investigate him. When he does, Tom gently leads the horse back to its stall.

It's funny where you can find God. We long to see him in thunder-and-lightning moments like we talked about yesterday. We want him to stand up in our boat and command the wind and the waves to "Be still!" as we saw him do last week. But sometimes the way God speaks into our lives looks more like "The Horse Whisperer" than Bruce Almighty. Sometimes his voice is so gentle and light that even the slightest distraction keeps us from hearing him. Yet, just like Tom, he waits until we are close enough, and then he opens his mouth and assures us—not with thunder and lightning but with his whisper—that all will be well.

Read 1 Kings 19:1-18

Fill in the blanks:
First Kings 19:11-12 says, "The LORD said, '_____ out and _____ on the mountain in the _____ of the _____, for the LORD is about to _____ by.' Then a great and powerful _____ tore the mountains apart and _____ the rocks before the LORD, but the _____ was not in the _____. After the _____ there was an _____, but the _____ was not in the _____. After the _____

came a _____, but the _____ was
not in the _____. And after the
_____ came a _____ _____."

■ **What does this passage tell you**
   about God?

_____

_____

   In this story we find the prophet Elijah in a desperate situation. He had
just seen God send fire down from heaven in his showdown with the
prophets of Baal at Mount Carmel. But now evil Queen Jezebel wanted
Elijah's head on a platter. So Elijah fled and questioned God and pretty much
threw a pity party for himself. It got so bad that Elijah told God he wanted
to die. At just the right time, in just the right place, and in just the right way,
God answered—but he did so in a way that catches many of us by surprise.
He didn't yell. He didn't come in fire, wind, or earthquake. He came in a whisper and assured Elijah that everything would be OK, encouraging Elijah that
just because he had been silent didn't mean that he hadn't been working.

■ **How is God wooing you with his whisper**
   today?

_____

_____

_____

■ **If God was speaking in a whisper to you**
   today, would you be able to hear him?
   ❑ **yes**
   ❑ **no**

Explain your answer.

_____

_____

Still yourself today. Find somewhere that is quiet and away from all distractions where you can spend thirty minutes. You may want to go for a walk, sit by a lake or go to your church's sanctuary. When you get there, don't say anything to God. Just sit, listen, meditate and think. Give God an opportunity to speak. Then spend some time journaling your thoughts below. It's OK if you don't sense God saying anything to you during these thirty minutes. Journal your thoughts anyway. The important thing is that you give God an opportunity to talk. Spending time in silence and solitude regularly means we are setting aside moments where we can intentionally listen for God's whisper.

_____

_____

_____

_____

_____

_____

_____

1 Chronicles
14:8-17

discerning
God's voice

■ How do you hear from God?

☐ through my friends
☐ through my pastor or youth leader
☐ through the Bible
☐ I listen for his voice.

We have spent a lot of time looking at and thinking about Job and the terrible things he went through. We've asked many questions about Job, God, and life. But we haven't spent much time looking at Job's interactions with his friends. Eliphaz, Bildad, Zophar, and Elihu say a lot in the book of Job. However, their advice for Job caused him a lot of pain. They had a lot of opinions about what Job is going through and why he was in a season of brokenness. The problem was that their advice came from their own words, not God's.

■ Have you ever experienced a time where it felt like your friends were out of touch and couldn't give you wisdom on what you were going through?

☐ yes
☐ no

If so, explain that situation.

_____

_____

_____

_____

Fill in the blanks:
First Chronicles 14:10 says, "So David
_____ of _____: 'Shall I
go and attack the Philistines? Will you
hand them over to me?' The LORD
_____ him, 'Go, I will hand them
over to you.'"

The Bible tells us that God never changes. He is the same yesterday, today, and forever. The God who was David's God is also your God. The same one who answered David is your Father if you are in Christ. Sometimes we forget that God wants to walk and talk with us, and as a result we do a whole lot of talking to God but not much listening. When we find ourselves in a bind or a season of brokenness, we run to our friends or our family or some book instead of stopping to talk to God about it. These things aren't bad, and God can show himself to us through them. But a problem arises when we fail to stop and listen to God or only pause for a moment and then go on with our lives and wonder why he is silent.

That's not the way it was for David. David asked God a question, and God answered him. One of the reasons is that David's pace of life was a lot different than ours. Noise and busyness surround us at all times. We have more distractions—TV, Internet, video games, music—than any people group in the history of the world. David faced distractions too, but he ordered his life so that he could hear God, and he waited for God to answer before he moved forward. If we want to hear God as David did, we must fix our hearts on him and learn to live in atmospheres that allow room for God to speak. The great truth is that God wants to speak to us more than we want to hear from him. The problem is that we don't put ourselves in position to listen often enough.

All of us go through seasons where we really need to hear a word from our Father. Our friends are great, and God can speak through them, but he wants to speak to us directly also. If we will quiet our hearts before him and be patient enough to hear him speak, we will find a relationship with him that we never thought possible. God wants us to hear him.

Take time to consider what people are saying about the brokenness around you right now. What are your friends saying? What are your parents saying? What are your church leaders saying? What is the culture saying? What are books saying? What is the Bible saying? Take some time to write down your answers to these questions. Then focus on what God is saying about the brokenness around you. Ask him to help you discern his voice as you sit in silence.

_____

_____

_____

_____

_____

_____

_____

he has
spoken

When I was eight years old, I really wanted a baseball glove. I was enthralled by the idea of having a glove, even though I wasn't much of a baseball player. I had seen a major leaguer talking on TV about the importance of learning the fundamentals of baseball, and it suddenly became important to me. So I pestered my dad for what seemed like ten years to get me a glove. As the weeks went by, I daydreamed about fielding grounders in the yard with my glove. But that dream never became a reality.

One day, I went into the garage for no particular reason and, like many eight-year-olds do, I found a big barrel and started digging through it. Imagine my shock when I found a baseball glove in there. I had no idea how the glove got there or whose it was. All I knew was that I was suddenly ready to play. It was strange to find something I had wanted for so long. What I sought after for weeks was already mine; I just didn't know I had it.

Yesterday's devotion talked about how God wants to speak to us as he spoke to David. If we will be still and listen, we will hear him on a consistent basis in our lives. At the same time, we must not overlook the fact that he has spoken to us through his Word. Many times, we wait on a word from God when there are thousands of words at our fingertips. The Bible is amazing, and if we will get into it and dig around, we will discover God's truth about who he is and who we are. I can't tell you how many times God has spoken to me through his word. It happens so often that it is natural to me now—not because I am a wonderful or spiritual person but because of who God is and what his Word is. God speaks to his people through his Word. When we are in seasons of brokenness, waiting on God to break through and speak, maybe he's not being silent. Maybe he's waiting on us to discover his words in the Bible.

■ Has God ever spoken to you through the Bible?
- ❑ yes
- ❑ no

If so, explain that situation.

_____

_____

_____

_____

■ How does God speak through his Word?

_____

_____

_____

_____

Read Psalm 119

Fill in the blanks:
Psalm 119:105 says, "Your _____ is a
_____ to my _____ and a
_____ for my _____."

Psalm 119 is David's expression of how much God's Word meant to him. Unlike David, we in today's world neglect the Bible far too often. People have committed their lives to the spread of this book and even lost their lives on its behalf. God's Word is powerful, and he will speak to us through it if we will take the time to study and meditate on and absorb it. Instead of embracing the Bible, though, we overlook it like I overlooked the baseball glove that was in the garage all along.

When you understand God's love for you, you grow in the desire to learn more about him. The Bible is a great place to go for that. It has been a beacon of light and love for countless Christians in seasons of brokenness, and it can be one for you, too. It is alive and active. God is waiting for us to ask him to speak to us through his word.

Spend some more time in Psalm 119 today and ask God to speak to you. Read slowly and allow God to tell you about who he is and who you are. He can speak into our brokenness like no one else, and one of the ways he does this is through his word. Give him room to speak to you through the Bible today.

the word
made flesh

Sometimes a simple action speaks louder than words ever could. Take for example the moment your dad gives you the look—you know the look— telling you what you just did will cost you later. Or what about the moment when you surprise your boyfriend or girlfriend with a gift that takes his/her breath away? All that person can do is sit there amazed. No words are said, and none are necessary.

A moment like this happened on November 3, 2002, in a football game between Marshall University and Akron University. Marshall's Byron Leftwich was one of the best college quarterbacks in the country and by far his team's best player. But less than ten minutes into the opening quarter, Leftwich suffered a severe ankle injury that knocked him out of the contest. Marshall, a big favorite in the game, fell behind 27-10 as Leftwich went to the hospital for X-rays. But after returning from the hospital, Leftwich insisted on going back into the game, even though he could hardly walk. In the third quarter, Leftwich returned to lead his team. It was an inspirational moment. No pep talks or words were necessary, because Leftwich's actions said more than words ever could. Leftwich's offensive linemen were so inspired by his courageous return that they tenaciously protected him. Two of these line-men, Steve Sciullo and Nate McPeek, carried Leftwich to the line of scrim-mage after every play. And even though the deficit in the game was too large for Marshall and Leftwich to overcome, the quarterback sent his teammates a message they would never forget by coming back.[1]

> ## Read John 1:1-18

Fill in the blanks:
John 1:14 says, "The _____ became _____ and _____ his _____ among us. We have _____ his _____, the glory of the _____ and _____, who came from the _____, full of _____ and _____."

- Put this verse in your own words using eight words or less.

_____

_____

- What does this passage tell you about God?

_____

_____

_____

_____

In one of the boldest and most gracious moves of all time, God became flesh and lived among us. Before Jesus came, Israel's history was marked by four hundred years of silence. John the Baptist inaugurated God's new work by prophesying about Jesus, but then Jesus burst onto the scene of human history in a stunning way. John 1 tells us that the same Word who made everything now had hands and feet. He tabernacled or dwelled among us and took our brokenness upon himself. We still hear this story being told through Scripture and in our churches today.

Jesus' coming to earth is a moment that speaks louder than words ever could. We no longer need to ask if God is active in our world, if God cares, or if our world is beyond his reach. The life of Jesus is God's greatest word for our lives. We need not be afraid of God's silence or even of brokenness in our lives. God has spoken so loudly through Jesus that, even if he never spoke again, it would be enough for the deepest tragedies of our lives.

prayer exercise:

Search the gospels today in an attitude of prayer and listen for what God wants to tell you through the life of Jesus. Listen carefully

to the Spirit's prompting as you
skim the gospels and review Jesus'
life. Allow the Spirit of God to
direct you to stories that embody
where you are right now. Watch Jesus
interact with both the characters in
the gospel and your life. Then use
the space provided below to journal
what you sense God is saying to you
today through Jesus' life.

_____

_____

_____

_____

_____

_____

_____

_____

_____

notes

1. Greg Perry, "Zips Drop Herd," (http://marshall.theinsiders.com), 11-3-02

_____

_____

_____

_____

_____

_____

_____

_____

_____

_____

_____

_____

_____

_____

This page is designed to give you space to take notes during your "Broken" group session or to journal your reflections on the highlights of this week's study.

WEEK SEVEN

seeing God in brokenness

where
questions fade

It is impossible for some things to live up to the hype preceding them. Movies are a great example. For every sequel actually worth watching, many more leave us disappointed. The Super Bowl usually is more hype than substance. How many times have we listened to weeks of interviews and trash talking only to see one team blow out the other in the big game? Dating can also be this kind of experience. How many times have your ideas about a person been shattered once the two of you actually spend time together? In a world where marketing companies exist to make products look better than they really are, it is hard for many things to live up to our expectations. But every once in a while, something comes along that does just that.

Last year, I had the rare opportunity to go to Cameron Indoor Stadium to watch the Duke Blue Devils take on the Georgia Tech Yellow Jackets in a basketball game. I had grown up watching Duke play on TV, so when my brother, a Duke graduate student, asked me if I wanted to go to the game and sit in the student section with him, it was the opportunity of a lifetime for me. I had heard about the atmosphere of Duke basketball games from commentators on TV. I had even toured the gym once during a visit to see my brother. But a tour or TV analyst could not prepare me for what I experienced inside Cameron that day. The fans at Duke take their team even more seriously than I first thought. Let's just say that watching a Duke game live is not a spectator sport. It's active. Had I known what was going to happen, I would have stretched beforehand. We stood all game. We cheered for Duke. We hounded the other team. It was almost as if everyone in the arena was being directed by an unseen hand. The students are so close to the court they can almost touch the players, and the organized chaos that ensued on every possession left me speechless and overwhelmed. The "Cameron Crazies" made this ordinary game phenomenal.

Read Job 42:1-6

```
Fill in the blanks:
Job 42:5-6 said, "My _____ had _____
of _____ but now my _____ have
_____ you. Therefore I _____ myself
and _____ in _____ and _____."
```

■ What is Job saying in these verses?

_____

_____

_____

■ How would you describe Job's reaction to God?

❑ shock   ❑ awe
❑ disinterest   ❑ disappointment

Last week we saw how God stepped into Job's brokenness and spoke. For chapter after chapter, God was silent. But at just the right time and in just the right way, God spoke. In chapter 42, we see Job's reaction to God. Needless to say, God lived up to the hype. In an Isaiah-like experience, Job was overwhelmed by God. In that moment, all Job's questions faded. Notice that God never told Job why he went through brokenness. God simply showed himself to Job, and that was enough. In the moment of God's revelation, questions of why were insignificant.

This brings us to the truth we will look at this week, that we see God in brokenness. There are some things about God we can only learn through brokenness. We know God as Healer only when we are sick. We know him as Comforter only in discomfort. We know him as Restorer only when we are in pieces. More than any other times in our lives, in these moments of deepest brokenness we see God most clearly.

What have you learned about God in this journey of brokenness that you could not have learned any other way?

_____

_____

_____

_____

_____

_____

Spend your prayer time today thinking about this question and asking God to reveal himself to you. Journal your answers as God speaks to you.

from head
to heart

Luke
24:13-49

Have you ever not been able to see something right in front of you? I'm not talking about being someplace that is so dark you can't see anything. I'm talking about having something right in front of your face on a bright sunny day that for some reason you just can't see. I have this experience every time I pick up a camera that is zoomed in all the way. I'll look through the lens but only see a dark spot. I put the camera down to make sure the thing in front of me hasn't moved, and it hasn't. But when I put the camera up to my eye again, all I see is a blur. I've had the same experience in every biology or physics lab I've ever been in. Someone would put something under the microscope for me to look at, but I couldn't see it. I'd check to make sure the slide hadn't moved, and it hadn't. But when I looked in the eyepiece, all I saw was a blur. So I did what every other student did in Biology lab. I bluffed and said, "Wow, that is so awesome!" and then let the next student take a turn.

I figured out a few years ago what had been happening to me all these years. In each instance, whether I was using a camera, a video camera or a microscope, I couldn't see the big picture. All I needed to do was zoom out, and the blur would become whatever was right in front of me. Think about all the frustration and wasted hours that could have been avoided had I moved a few fingers.

Read Luke 24:13-49

■ Re-tell this story in your own words.

_____

_____

_____

■ What problem did the men on the road to Emmaus and the disciples in the upper room have in common?

_____

_____

_____

■ What was the answer to their problem?
❏ They needed to be healed.
❏ They needed money.
❏ They needed to have their minds opened.

We catch this fascinating story mid-scene as two followers of Jesus walked on the road to Emmaus discussing what had happened the previous weekend. Jesus had been crucified. Their hope that he was the Messiah had vanished. Needless to say, they were in a moment of brokenness. The one whom they left all to follow had died. All their efforts and sacrifices seemed to be in vain. But as they walked and discussed these events, Jesus caught up with them and joined the conversation. Beside the two men walked the resurrected Lord, but they didn't recognize him. Only later when he broke bread did they see who he was. In a similar way, Jesus' disciples in the upper room needed their minds to be opened to understand Jesus' mission and why he had to die.

It's interesting to think about this story. Here were people who knew the Scriptures but missed the God of the Scriptures who had been in their midst. They knew the word but missed the Word. Their heads were trained, but their hearts were blinded. God was standing right in front of them, but they missed him. They needed their minds to be opened so they could understand the Scriptures.

It's possible for us as well to have God in our midst but miss him totally. You may have found yourself complaining that God never reveals himself to you when in reality he is standing right in front of you. It's easy to be so zoomed into our own lives that we miss God right in front of us. Even more, we can be so consumed with thinking about God or trying to figure him out that we miss him in our hearts. We need God's Spirit to open our minds and hearts so we too can recognize God. We need more than head knowledge of him. We need the kind of heart knowledge that leaves us responding as Job did: overwhelmed, awed, repentant, and amazed.

prayer exercise:

What would it look like for you to look for God with both your head and heart?

_____

_____

_____

Have you engaged your heart in your search for God in brokenness? God calls you to do so. Ask the Spirit today to open your mind and heart so that you can see God.

only part
of the story

It's impossible to go through life without going through hard times. Life is difficult, and sometimes we go through seasons of brokenness. None of us is immune to difficult life situations. One of the reasons we wrote this book was to be honest about this.

But if we are not careful, we will find ourselves constantly focusing on the tough times. It's easy to wallow in pain because we find some comfort in doing so. It takes real courage to proclaim that you will trust God to bring you through brokenness.

The longer you walk with God, the more you come to realize that brokenness is only part of the story. It's not the end. For Christians, brokenness will never have the last word. Even in death, we will find Jesus waiting with open arms to receive us into his eternal kingdom. Whatever difficult situation we find ourselves in, we can rest assured that it will not have the final say in our lives.

Read Genesis 22:1-19

■ What do you think was going through Abraham's mind when God called him to sacrifice Isaac? (Check all that apply.)

❏ disbelief   ❏ panic   ❏ resignation
❏ anger   ❏ peace   ❏ trust

■ What would you have been thinking if you were in Abraham's situation?

_____

_____

_____

■ Would you describe Abraham as broken in this situation?

☐ yes
☐ no

Why or why not?

_____

_____

_____

_____

This is one of the most familiar stories in the Bible, but every time we read it, we feel the emotions of it just as vividly. It had been a miracle for Abraham and Sarah to get pregnant and have a son. When God called Abraham to kill that son, Isaac, as a sacrifice, it must have wrecked him. It's easy for us to speed through this part of the story because we know the ending. But Abraham couldn't speed through it. Imagine the heart-rending emotions that he must have felt. Somewhere in the night, he had to wonder what God was doing and why he was doing it. Even through those questions, though, Abraham trusted God. That didn't make obedience any easier, but Abraham chose to be faithful. And in the end, God stepped in and completely changed the situation by providing a ram to be the sacrifice in Isaac's place. Abraham learned that God provides, and he named the mountain "the LORD will provide" to celebrate this truth about God he could only learn through brokenness.

God calls us to trust him as Abraham did. As we do, we need to learn as Abraham did that brokenness is not the final word in our lives. God loves to speak into the middle of our toughest situations. It thrilled God's heart to see Abraham trust him, and it thrills God's heart when we do the same. God has not changed—he will be the same God for us that he was for Abraham. We just have to trust him and believe that brokenness is not the end for us. Things may look bleak for a season, even a long one, but at some point God will break through and heal our situations as he did for Abraham and Isaac. We can take comfort as we trust him in difficult times.

■ How does this story of Abraham and Isaac give you comfort?

_____

_____

_____

■ What is the significance of the fact that brokenness does not have the final say in your life?

_____

_____

_____

prayer exercise:

Today, praise God for having the final say in your life. Brokenness is not the entire story. Call to him and declare to him how wonderful he is to you. Even if your emotions are totally opposite of this truth right now, go against them and speak the truth of who God is to him and to your heart.

when seeing
means limping

I can now see that it was the best worst day of my life.

Earlier in the book, I told the story of how I blew out the anterior cruciate ligament in my knee. Two years later, it happened again, as I tore the ACL a second time. Many of my hopes and dreams died on an operating table that March morning years ago. Six months of pain, rehab and questions about God followed this moment. I still suffer from that day today. The pain is fresh in my mind every time I go to watch a college soccer game. I'm reminded of my weakness every time I play in a pick up basketball game and hang around the perimeter instead of driving through the lane. Every time it gets cold, the weather changes, or I sit in a cramped position in a car for too long, the injury nags me again. And every time I hear someone give easy, thoughtless, Sunday School answers to difficult life questions, I cringe. Yet through it all, the things I learned about God in my season of brokenness have changed me for the better.

Isn't it interesting when people talk about the most difficult times in their lives as the most meaningful? I know that is true for me. As I write this devotion, almost ten years later, I can see that one of the worst seasons of my life has also been one of the best. One of the passages of Scripture that has impacted me most personally is the story of Jacob wrestling with God, because that's exactly what I experienced in brokenness.

Read Genesis 32:22-32

■ Re-tell the story in your own words in the space provided below.

_____

_____

_____

■ What happened when God touched Jacob's hip?

- ☐ He healed the hip.
- ☐ He made the hip more powerful.
- ☐ He wrenched the hip and left Jacob with a limp.

■ How was Jacob changed by this moment of brokenness?

_____

_____

_____

Martin Luther called this passage of Scripture one of the most disturbing in the entire Bible. In it, we see Jacob's struggle as he found himself caught between his past and his future. Jacob, the lifelong deceiver (his name can be translated "heel catcher" or "deceiver"), was in a precarious situation. His life looked like it could come crashing down at any moment. Laban was on one side, and Esau was on the other. Jacob was exposed. And what did God do? He jumped into Jacob's life and made it worse. Throughout the night, the two wrestled, until God put his finishing move on Jacob, and Jacob's hip was wrenched out of socket. Like The Rock™ going to the People's Elbow, God dropped the Immobilizer on Jacob, and in that moment of brokenness Jacob realized whom he was struggling against. Jacob spent the rest of the night holding on for dear life.

Jacob emerged from the encounter with God shaken, limping, and changed. He called the place *Peniel,* which means "the face of God." It was in this moment of brokenness that God had journeyed closest to Jacob. God was so close that he had even touched Jacob. By touching Jacob, God both wounded and healed him in the same motion. While Jacob walked away from that night with a limp, he also walked away with a new name and new mission. Jacob the deceiver would now be called Israel, which means **one who has struggled with God.** An entire nation took on this man's new identity.

As I have emerged from my own struggle with God, I still find myself limping, sometimes literally. I have never had many of my questions fully answered. But one thing I know for sure is that in brokenness I met God in a way I will always remember. I still carry scars. The pain is still very real on some days. But in the end, I know that God is good. I know that for Christians every death comes with a resurrection. Since my second injury, my mission too has been changed, which is one reason you are reading this book today.

prayer exercise:

Take some time today to imagine your life ten years from now. What will it look like? What do you think you will have learned about God from this season in your life? How do you think your direction will change, if it will change at all? Use the space below to journal your thoughts as you ask God to help you imagine yourself on the other side of your journey.

_____

_____

_____

_____

_____

_____

_____

when wounds
heal

Job
42:7-17

In 1463, leaders of the city of Florence, Italy, wanted to place a statue out-side city hall that reflected the city's beauty and strength The city commis-sioned a sculptor named Agostino di Duccio to complete the project. Agostino went to the quarry to have a piece of white marble nineteen feet long cut for his masterpiece. But the marble was cut too shallow, and it fell when it was removed, leaving a deep fracture down one side of the stone. Agostino deemed the piece of marble unusable and demanded another, but the city council refused. As a result, the cracked marble sat unused for thirty-eight years, a source of embarrassment for all concerned.

In 1501, another sculptor came on the scene. He took the piece of marble Agostino had deemed unusable into his workshop and worked for three years chiseling and polishing it. He finally emerged with a statue of David relaxing after defeating Goliath. Michelangelo Buonarroti's work was stun-ning. The statue was so huge that it took forty-nine men five days to move it to the front of city hall. Roads were widened and buildings torn down to make way for the statue. In the 500 years since then, people have come from all over the world to admire Michelangelo's work of art.[1]

Read Job 42:7-17

■ Compare Job's possessions in chapter 42 with his possessions in chapter 1. What happened?

❑ God gave Job back all of his possessions.

❑ God doubled Job's possessions.

■ How did Job act in this passage toward the friends who criticized him?

_____

_____

_____

■ How would you have acted in a similar situation?

_____

_____

_____

Restoration is a beautiful thing. Just as Michelangelo beautifully restored the slab of marble, God restored Job in chapter 42. Job's possessions were doubled. He was given more children. His world was set right. He was vindicated. God's hand of blessing returned. And although Job always bore the scars from his season of brokenness, his story has been told throughout the ages. He is known as a beacon of hope in a world where brokenness has become normal. He is forever remembered as a faithful follower of God.

The thing that impresses me most about Job is the way he acted in restoration. Once Job was restored, he didn't use his vindication to get back at his friends. He didn't carry a chip on his shoulder. Job didn't look to cause others the same kind of suffering he endured. Rather, Job walked in his world as a wounded healer, offering hope, intercession, and friendship to others in need. He becomes the perfect picture of leadership—one broken man who has been restored mending the wounds of other broken people in his broken world.

One of my favorite communicators of God's word, Louie Giglio, made this statement: "In the end it is all good, so if it is not all good, it is not the end." This is the hope we come to this week. Restoration is the hope of all believers. Not even death can stop God from finishing his work in our lives. But our restoration should never stop with us. Once we emerge from our seasons of brokenness, we must not forget what we learned in the desert. When we experience restoration, we must become agents of restoration to others. We must intercede for our friends and our world. We must become people of hope and friendship. We must lead as wounded healers, not ungrateful tyrants. We must reveal in the light what we have learned in the dark.

```
Fill in the blanks:
In Matthew 10:27, Jesus says, "What I
_____ you in the _____, _____ in the
_____; what is _____ in your
_____, _____ from the
_____."
```

prayer exercise:

```
Ask God to show you today how you can
be a wounded healer in your community.
Commit to God today that as he
restores you—however and whenever he
chooses to do so—you will use your
restoration to offer intercession,
hope and friendship to others.
```

notes

1. Sam Whatley, *Pondering the Journey* (True Life Publishers, 2002) 17–18.

_____

_____

_____

_____

_____

_____

_____

_____

_____

_____

_____

_____

_____

_____

_____

This page is designed to give you space to take notes during your "Broken" group session or to journal your reflections on the highlights of this week's study.

WEEK EIGHT

seeing brokenness
through God

misconceptions
of brokenness

Is there anything worse than studying for a test? I would rather get run over by a golf cart than study for an exam. The only thing worse than studying for a test is studying for three of them in two days. I remember in my school days dreaming about the day when I would not have to study for any more tests. (Now I have book deadlines instead.)

The thing about studying for tests is that if you do your work, you will usually get a grade reflecting your preparation. For the most part, the harder you study, the better the score. But there are times when you study as hard as you possibly can—only to make an average or below-average grade on the test. I hated it when I put the work into learning something and still only made a C-minus. When this happens, you have to be honest with yourself, because you are the only one who knows whether you worked hard. But if you can look in the mirror and say you studied as hard and as long as you could and still did not make a good grade on the test, you get frustrated, and rightfully so. Normally, good old-fashioned hard work leads to a good grade, but sometimes it doesn't work that way.

■ **In what other areas of your life have you seen this phenomenon happen?**

_____

_____

_____

_____

_____

_____

- **Have you ever felt like this was happening in your relationship with God?**
  - ☐ yes
  - ☐ no

Explain your answer.

_____

_____

_____

_____

- **Why do you follow Jesus?**

_____

_____

_____

_____

During the days of Job, there was a prevailing opinion that if someone followed God and obeyed his commands, God would bless him, but if someone didn't walk with God or disobeyed his commands, he would be cursed. This theology is not completely wrong. It is true that God's blessings normally follow the obedient. It is true that bad things often happen as a result of disobedience. The problem comes when we expect this cause-and-effect reasoning to fit every situation. It's like studying for a test. While studying usually determines a grade, sometimes you make a bad grade even after studying hard and long.

Job's life shows us an exception to cause-and-effect theology. Job served and worshiped God, but brokenness still came his way. His story shows us that loving God with all that we are doesn't exempt us from brokenness. We can be living lives surrendered to God and still experience the kinds of things Job did. While blessings usually follow the obedient, it does not always work that way.

Job's friends rebuked him because their view of his situation was greatly influenced by cause-and-effect theology. But God had something to say to them at the end of the story.

Read Job 42:7-9

■ Contrast this passage with what Eliphaz said in Job 4:1-9.

Job's friends kept asking him what he had done wrong to deserve the punishment he was apparently getting from God. In their minds, Job must have done something terrible to bring this brokenness upon him. But God answered them and showed his displeasure with what they were saying. In doing so, he corrected their misconception of brokenness. We must be careful not to fall into the same trap as Eliphaz and company.

prayer exercise:

Examine your own season of brokenness through the perspective we've talked about today. Ask God to show you how you should look at your life. Maybe you have been walking in disobedience and you need to ask for forgiveness. Maybe you have been following God the best you can yet still find yourself in a tough season. Either way, ask God to reveal himself to you and praise him for who he is.

trusting
his heart

My grandparents lived on Lake Tobesofkee in Macon, Georgia, when I was growing up, and I went there every summer to spend several days on the water. I was swimming with my siblings and cousins one blazing hot summer day when I was twelve years old. On this particular day, we decided to swim into the cove further than we ever had before. Since I was the oldest in the group, I figured I should set the bar and head into the deep waters first. You know how it is when you're trying to show off. Suddenly you think you're a daredevil like Evel Knievel, and you try to be something you're not. That's what I did on this day.

Before I knew it, I was so far out in the water that I panicked. I turned around to see where everyone else was, and it seemed as though they were one hundred yards behind me. I got scared. I had no more energy to swim, and a fear of drowning started to take over. I started flailing about in the water. I thought the water there was at least 30 feet deep. I had no idea what to do, so I started screaming for help.

I stopped kicking for a moment and let my legs down when a funny thing happened. Suddenly, my feet hit a sandbar, and I realized I could stand up where I was. I breathed a sigh of relief as I realized I could stand. I could barely stick my nose out of the water, but at least I was safe.

■ Describe a time in your life when you were in a situation and wondered how you would get out of it.

_____

_____

_____

_____

■ What are we supposed to do when we can't make sense of our circumstances and don't know what to do?

_____

_____

_____

■ What does God call us to do in those situations?

_____

_____

Read Daniel 6

Sometimes things just don't make sense. Daniel's story is a perfect example. He was worshiping God, and it got him thrown into a lion's den. Talk about a sticky situation. What are you supposed to do when you are locked in a lion's den? We all know that Daniel did something quite extraordinary. When he could not see the hand of God in his situation, he trusted God nevertheless. This is a powerful truth to meditate on. Sometimes we flail away in a lake, wondering how we're going to make it, panicking over what to do, while all along there has been a sandbar right under our feet. Daniel could not make sense about where he was, but he trusted God. In our tough seasons and circumstances, we also have the choice to trust God's heart even when we can't see his hand.

■ What inspires you about Daniel's story?

_____

_____

■ How does the truth of Daniel's story affect your life?

_____

_____

_____

_____

prayer exercise:

Perhaps you are in a situation in life like the one I experienced in the lake. You may be scared or confused, and you may not know what to do. If that is the case, try to trust God's heart today even though you can't see his hand. If you will do this, you will find his character and goodness serving as your sandbar. God knows exactly what is going on with you, and he won't let you drown even if his answer isn't what you want and doesn't come when you want. Pour your heart out to him today and share your needs with him. He loves you and cares about your life.

the battle
beyond us

Not long ago, I went through a season in my life I just did not understand. It started off with nightmares. I'd never really had many nightmares before, but during this season I had them every single night. I asked my wife about it, and then she started having them too. They were awful for both of us. We often woke up screaming. We didn't know what in the world to do as this went on for two months.

Finally, one day I pleaded with God to show me what to do. I was surprised by his answer. Growing up, I was never taught much about the enemy to our faith. I never really focused on this issue, to be honest, because it was uncomfortable to think about, and I just didn't know that much about it. But the Lord showed me that the enemy was trying to scare me and keep me in bondage to fear. When God told me this and opened my eyes to who I am in Christ and the power I have in him, the fear began to leave, and the nightmares stopped. It had never even occurred to me that my nightmares were the result of spiritual warfare. Yet God spoke and showed me what to do. I'm not saying that every nightmare is of Satan, but I do know that for me in that season, that was the source.

■ Have you ever been through a situation that God showed you was an attack from the enemy?

❑ yes
❑ no

If so, describe that situation.

_____

_____

_____

_____

■ **What are we to do in the face of an attack from Satan?**

_____

_____

Read Ephesians 6:10-18

Paul uses some picturesque language here as he describes the war we are fighting in as followers of Jesus Christ. Now let me say this up front: I believe one of the most abused teachings in the body of Christ is on spiritual warfare. But that does not mean we face no battles. Satan wants to destroy us. He will try to come at us with whatever he can to take us off the course of following Christ. However, Jesus has stripped Satan of his authority (Colossians 2:15). Satan is not left to do anything he wants.

One of the major ways Satan comes at us as Christians is by infiltrating our thinking. If he can hold us in bondage and fear there, he can immobilize us. The ways we think can leave us paralyzed and defeated. Only when we take hold of the truth of who we are in Christ can we start to experience freedom.

Fill in the blanks:
John 8:32 says, "Then you will _____ the _____, and the _____ will set you _____."

Job was in the midst of spiritual warfare. Satan wanted to destroy his faith, and as a result Job experienced severe brokenness. Satan is real, and he seeks to destroy us as well. But just as with Job, this is not the last word. Jesus is our victorious king who has provided a way out for us. He defeated Satan on the cross. If we would get in the Word and learn who we are in Christ and how he has defeated Satan, we would not be so inclined to fear the enemy. If you are in a tough season and find yourself under assault, get in the Word and see what God has to say about it. Jesus tells us to take heart because he has overcome the world. Hang on to him in the midst of whatever you are going through. He will see you through. There is power in the name of Jesus.

Ask the Lord to show you if there are any areas of your life you need to give to him. Are you living in fear of anything? Do you need Jesus to show you who you are in him? Praise God for defeating Satan at the cross. Ask him to open your eyes to the reality of this victory in your life.

Jesus
and brokenness

The longer I walk with Jesus, the more I appreciate him. He has become so much more than a doctrine or thought process to me. He is not a think-tank; he is my best friend. I walk with him and talk with him on a daily basis. There was a time in my life when I struggled to get into the Word and absorb all of who my God is. I'm embarrassed to admit it, but I was doing a lot of preaching without actually abiding in him. I talked to him when it was convenient, and every now and then I would read a little here and there in the Bible. Not so anymore.

I've tried to figure out why my heart has changed. I believe it's because I've gotten a clearer picture of his love for me and of what he went through on this earth. None of us will go through life without going through hard times. But when we get into the Word, we see that Jesus went through tough times also. He knows what it's like to be broken. His body was broken for you and me!

Often it's easy for us to become self-absorbed when we go through diffi-cult things. When we do, we forget Jesus himself went through the same things. He knows what it is like to hurt. He knows what it is like to be left alone. He knows pain and misery. He can relate to us in our brokenness. He will be a best friend to us if we will let him. No one can relate to our broken-ness like Jesus can. Jesus was tested and tried just as we are. We have a God we can relate to in both the good and bad times of our lives.

Fill in the blanks:
Hebrews 4:15 says, "For we do not have a _____ _____ who is unable to sympa-thize with our _____, but we have one who has been tempted in every way, _____ as _____ _____—yet was without sin."

Notice how Isaiah's description of the coming Messiah paints such a vivid picture of his suffering on earth. The prophecy came true—Jesus experienced much grief, sorrow, and pain on earth. Think about him in the Garden of Gethsemane. Think of him on the Cross. Jesus understands our brokenness because even he was not exempt from it.

Instead of running from times of brokenness, maybe we should embrace them and learn from the God who went through desperate times as well. Jesus was not immune to brokenness, and neither are we. Thank God that he does not leave us on our own to deal with our problems, that our Deliverer understands exactly what we are going through.

■ How does a basic knowledge of what Jesus suffered bring you comfort in your hard times?

_____

_____

_____

_____

■ What hope does Jesus' suffering bring you in your brokenness?

_____

_____

_____

_____

Talk to Jesus today about the brokenness he experienced. Ask him to
remind you through the Word about the
hardships he encountered. Thank him
for being broken for you. Praise him
and rejoice in what he did for you.

the other
side of brokenness

We started our study through the book of Job with the story of broken-ness from one family in our community who lost their son, Clay, in a tragic boating accident. Today, we present the rest of this family's story. The account once again is told by Clay's mother, Linda Spencer.

God had everything under control; there is no other explanation. It was Clay's appointed time to be with God. I remember thinking that he could have been far away at Scout camp, and we could have gotten a phone call, but instead Clay died at home, doing what he loved with people he loved—and we were blessed to have our church family right by our side to comfort us.

As we looked back, the pieces started to fit together. God had been preparing us. He had given us incredible opportunities. We needed to focus on what God had given instead of what he had taken. Clay and I were able to take a cruise together, just the two of us. For spring break, Clay and his dad had spent the week in New York City alone for just some guy time together. The last year, our family trips had been the best ever.

I remembered my devotion for that day had dealt with death. Looking back at Clay's devotion book, we were shocked to see it was about dying also. It was actually titled, "Things Are Gonna Change." We knew we had to trust God with this. He loved us enough to give Clay to us in the first place, and this was just part of his plan. But that was easier said than done.

As long as we live on this earth, the Bible clearly states that there will be things we just simply cannot understand. We made the deci-sion to trust God, and with his grace we found peace—not under-standing. We started thanking God for the good things that we were able to find through the haze. We realized why Clay had gotten to do so much in such a short life. Just weeks earlier, Clay had seen my dri-ver's license and made the decision to be an organ donor. The last thing he did before the church group arrived was to give his younger brother a treasured possession he had been asking for.

His casket was so cool—he would have loved it. It was light wood, and with markers everyone was able to sign it and write things to him. The evening of the funeral we noticed that the moon was in the shape of a banana (crescent) with only one star in the sky. We felt as if Clay were shining down on us.

We tried to think of what we could do to remember Clay, praise God and give back to the community. But not in our wildest dreams did we ever imagine that we could pull off building a park. But with a little faith, everything is possible. There was a beautiful piece of land at the public boat landing. It had a view of the mountains, sunset, and lake and was a favorite place for Clay and his dad to ride bikes. After much prayer, we approached the water works with our plan to build a park. They were cooperative and excited with our idea. We poured our heart and soul into the next ten months designing and purchasing the equipment. It was a great way to channel our energy and grief.

May 24, 2003, was another beautiful day in South Carolina. This was the day we dedicated Anchor Park. It would have been Clay's thirteenth birthday. He would have loved it. Now, every time we pass it and see the children playing, we thank God for letting this dream come together, for the opportunity to be a part of his wonderful plan and for never leaving our side. The anchor and the marker at the park say it best: "Hope is symbolized in Christian iconography by an anchor. And what does the anchor do? It keeps the ship on course when the wind and the waves ravage against it. But the anchor of hope is sunk in heaven, not on earth."

There may be no greater place for us to end our study of brokenness than in Romans 8. The hope of this passage has mended the wounds of Christians for centuries.

Read Romans 8:18-39

- Pick one verse from this passage that describes your journey through this book and rewrite it in your own words.

_____

_____

■ How does this passage describe your
journey through brokenness over the
last eight weeks?

_____

_____

_____

The great news about God is he always finishes his stories. He becomes strength in our weakness. He makes good from bad. He stands beside us in our questions and reveals himself to us in our brokenness. We cannot say just what God will do through the brokenness you have encountered in your life. We do not end this study with easy answers or empty promises that there will never be any more pain. But we can say with assurance that in the end, there is no brokenness beyond his reach.

prayer exercise:

Go through your journal entries in this book and review what God has showed you through this study. Look through the book at the things you underlined and the notes that you made. Thank God for the things he has showed you about himself and find rest in his goodness. Meditate on your journey and sense his peace that passes all understanding.

This page is designed to give you space to take notes during your "Broken" group session or to journal your reflections on the highlights of this week's study.

BROKEN
About the Authors

CHAD NORRIS

Chad is a speaker and writer who desires to lead people in their spiritual journeys to become loving followers of Jesus Christ. In this calling, he speaks to children, students, and adults in a variety of settings and writes several resources. Chad is a co-founder of Wayfarer Ministries and serves as one of the weekly teachers for Engage, a praise and worship Bible study for 20-somethings in upstate South Carolina. After graduating from the University of Georgia in 1995, Chad received his Master of Divinity from Beeson Divinity School in 2000. Chad's love of the journey and realistic viewpoints help nurture people in their personal spiritual  growth. This is the fourth book Chad has co-authored in the Following God for Youth series. Chad, wife Wendy, and son Sam live in Greer, SC.

DAVID RHODES

As a speaker and author, David has a passion to help people rediscover life as followers of Jesus Christ. His creative, challenging, and honest approach encour-ages a variety of individuals and groups in various ministry settings. David is a co-founder of Wayfarer Ministries and one of the weekly speakers at Engage, a praise-and-worship Bible study for 20-somethings in upstate South Carolina. David graduated from Palm Beach Atlantic University in 1996 and earned his Master of Divinity from Beeson Divinity School in 2000. This is the fourth book David has co-authored in the Following God for Youth series. David, wife Kim, and daughter Emma live near Greenville, SC.

For more information about the authors of this study, please contact:
Wayfarer Ministries
1735 John B. White Sr. Blvd.
Suite 9, Box 201
Spartanburg, SC 29301-5462
www.wayfarerministries.org

notes

notes

notes